Découpage the Easy Way

PLAID®

Découpage
the Easy Way

Sterling Publishing Co., Inc. New York
A Sterling / Chapelle Book

Chapelle, Ltd.:
- Owner: Jo Packham
- Editor: Laura Best
- Staff: Ann Bear, Areta Bingham, Kass Burchett, Marilyn Goff, Holly Hollingsworth, Susan Jorgensen, Barbara Milburn, Linda Orton, Karmen Quinney, Leslie Ridenour, Cindy Stoeckl, Gina Swapp, Sara Toliver

Plaid Enterprises:
- Editor: Mickey Baskett
- Staff: Sylvia Carroll, Jeff Herr, Laney McClure, Dianne Miller, Jerry Mucklow, Phyllis Mueller

If you have any questions or comments, please contact:
Chapelle, Ltd., Inc., P.O. Box 9252, Ogden, UT 84409
(801) 621-2777 • (801) 621-2788 Fax
chapelle@chapelleltd.com • www.chapelleltd.com

Library of Congress Cataloging-in-Publication Data Available

10 9 8 7 6 5 4 3 2

First paperback edition published in 2002 by
Sterling Publishing Company, Inc.
387 Park Avenue South, New York, N.Y. 10016
©2001 by Plaid Enterprises
Distributed in Canada by Sterling Publishing
c/o Canadian Manda Group, One Atlantic Avenue, Suite 105
Toronto, Ontario, Canada M6K 3E7
Distributed in Great Britain by Chrysalis Books
64 Brewery Road. London N7 9NT. England
Distributed in Australia by Capricorn Link (Australia) Pty. Ltd.
P.O. Box 704, Windsor, NSW 2756 Australia

Printed and Bound in China
All Rights Reserved

Sterling ISBN 0-8069-3637-1
0-8069-7359-5

Introduction

What Is Découpage?

Découpage is the art of decorating objects with cut-out pictures and printed designs, then adding a glass-like finish to cover, seal, and protect them. The term comes from the old French word découper, which means "to cut out." The origins of this art can be traced to 18th-century Italy. From there, it spread to England and northern Europe. In the 19th century, fashionable ladies on the continent used embossed and die-cut designs as ornaments for boxes, screens, panels, and furniture.

During the first half of the 20th century and into the 1960s, découpage was a popular craft, despite the fact that it took many long hours to achieve a refined finish. Up to thirty coats of lacquer were applied to boxes, plaques, and wooden purses, with much sanding and polishing to achieve a glass-like finish.

With today's water-based finishes, prints can be applied and an attractive finish can be achieved in no time. This book shows you how to create découpage on a variety of surfaces and contains a treasure trove of ideas from several talented designers. The projects are fun, fast, and particularly suitable for beginners.

With découpage, there is no limit to the type of items you can create. Select a surface; choose a favorite print, photograph, or memento; follow the easy technique steps and—voila, you will have created a keepsake. Gifts, home decor items, picture frames, keepsake boxes, personalized treasures, and more are possible with découpage. A child's artwork, a favorite photograph, a theatre playbill, a wine label, or a lovely greeting card can be the beginning of a creation that will have lasting meaning.

Table of Contents

General Supplies

Découpage Finish

When doing your découpage projects, be certain to use a finish made especially for découpage. This type of finish is designed to use for both gluing and coating the prints. It contains solids and dryers to achieve a thick buildup that dries quickly. This type of finish also is self-leveling so the finish will dry smoothly.

Découpage finishes provide great results on a variety of surfaces. Two coats are sufficient to protect and submerge the prints. More coats can be added for a thick buildup of finish. A thick built-up finish can be sanded to a smooth finish. Découpage finish provides a hard finish that has superior water resistance.

All-in-One Glue/Sealer/Finish is a type of finish especially suitable for porous surfaces such as terra-cotta, plastic foam, and working with candles and fabrics. It seals wood, paper, and prints; it glues paper, fabric, and other porous materials; and it protects stains, acrylic paints, and découpage prints. It is nontoxic and permanent and it dries quick and clear. Découpage finish is available in matte and gloss sheens. A variety of sizes are also available in both sheens. Either of the above types of finishes can be used as the top finish coat for your découpage project.

Photograph transfer medium is a terrific way to display a favorite photograph or print on fabric. Black-and-white or color photocopies can be easily and permanently transferred onto fabric. Photograph transfer medium comes in clear (for use on white fabrics) and opaque (for use on colored fabrics).

Aerosol sealers are convenient and available in gloss or matte finishes. Spray-on finishes can be used when a thick buildup of finish is not required. They can be used to quickly seal a print or a surface before applying the découpage finish. They can also be used after the buildup of finish to create a high shine or pearl finish. Choose sealers that are nonyellowing and quick-drying. If project is too shiny after finish coats are dry, buff with a fine-grade steel wool or water-moistened 400-grit sandpaper.

If project is made of new wood and was stained or glazed, the wood is rather porous; therefore, the surface will soak up most of the first coat or finish, requiring more coats than a painted surface.

A piece that will receive a lot of use, or will be used outdoors, will need more finish coats for protection.

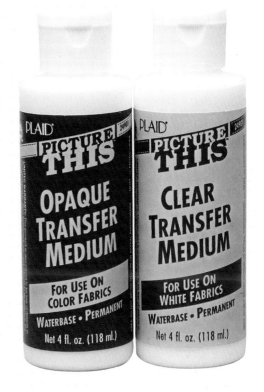

Paints for Découpage

Acrylic craft paints—are premixed, richly pigmented, flat finish paints that come ready to use. These high-quality paints are available in a huge range of colors, including rich metallics. These paints can be used to base-coat surfaces before painting designs, as well as to do the actual design painting.

Stencil gel paints—are semitranslucent stenciling paints that offer maximum control and blending ability. They are formulated to enhance the intricate detail of stenciling, especially when shading designs. The transparent colors blend with ease to give depth to every design. They are water-based and fast-drying. The thicker gel formula prevents runs and does not leave hard edges of paint build-up. Stencil gel paints are also available in a wide variety of colors.

Découpage Supplies

Brushes—used for all painting, brushes are made from either synthetics or animal hair. Synthetic brushes are made especially for use with acrylic paints. Brushes are designed for specific purposes:

- Liners are used for small detail and lettering.
- Flat brushes are used for base-coating and painting designs.
- Fan brushes are used for a wispy coverage.
- Sponge brushes are used for base-coating and applying découpage finish.
- Stencil brushes have densely packed natural bristles for smooth, soft blending.

10

Sandpaper, 220-grit—for sanding wood, terra-cotta, and tin before painting.

Sea sponges—when slightly moistened, can be used to create texture and blend colors.

Sharp, small scissors or craft knife—for cutting prints.

Soft cloth— to wipe away dust and excess antiquing medium or glaze. It is also used for wiping brushes since rough paper towels can damage brushes.

Steel wool #0000 and 400-grit sandpaper—for polishing the finish.

Straightedge or metal ruler—to ensure straight, smooth cuts.

Tack cloth—used for removing sanding dust. Tack the surface after every sanding.

Glazing medium—is a translucent medium available in an array of colors, which can be mixed with acrylic paint to achieve a wide range of tones. This thins down the paint and makes the paint translucent. The mixture can also be used to stain unfinished wood or to antique a painted surface.

Painting Supplies & Tools

Eraser—for removing slight smudges.

Palette or disposable foam plates—for holding and mixing paints.

Palette knife—to mix and apply paint. Palette knives come in two styles. Both have long, flat blades, but one type has an elevated handle to help keep your hand out of the paint. A good palette knife should be thin and flexible when it touches the project surface.

Stylus—used to transfer a traced design onto a prepared surface. A pencil or ballpoint pen that no longer writes may also be used.

Tracing paper—used for tracing a design or pattern. Choose a tracing paper that is as transparent as possible for carefully tracing designs.

Transfer paper—used to transfer a traced design or pattern to the project surface. Choose transfer paper that has a water-soluble coating in a color that will be visible on the base-coat color of the project surface. Position the design on the project surface. Secure with low-tack masking tape. Slip the transfer paper, velvet side down, between the tracing and the project surface. Use a stylus to retrace the pattern lines, using enough pressure to transfer the lines but not so much as to indent the surface.

Waxed paper—to cover your work surface.

Brush Accessories

Water container & clean water—to rest the brush in. Keep the ferrule and handle out of the water. A container with a ridged bottom helps clean the bristles.

Brush cleaner—to clean wet or dried paint from bristles, and groom brush between uses.

General Instructions

Selecting Prints

Design motifs to découpage can be found in a variety of forms. Select designs from art prints, gift wrap, postcards, greeting cards, memorabilia, dried flowers and leaves, fabrics, or photographs. Even magazines, newspapers, and other print media can be used.

Using Photocopies

It is often more convenient to use black-and-white or color photocopies of memorabilia such as playbills, tickets, and pressed flowers. The copies will be easier to work with and you preserve the original. Photocopy machines can be found at grocery stores, libraries, quick-print shops, and many other places. However, do not make photocopies of copyrighted material.

Using Photographs

Black-and-white or color photocopies are the best and easiest way to use photographs for découpage—the thinner copy paper is easier to work with than photographic paper, and you can keep your photographs intact. Only make photocopies of photographs you have taken yourself. Do not use other people's photographs without their permission.

Tracing & Transferring Patterns

Patterns for projects in this book are located on pages surrounding the project's instructions. To keep the patterns intact, trace designs onto tracing paper.

Place tracing paper over design or pattern sheet. Secure with low-tack masking tape. With a permanent marking pen or pencil, trace main lines of pattern. Transfer designs onto the project surface, using transfer paper and a stylus.

Preparing Surfaces

Wood, candles, papier-maché, terra-cotta, tin, plastic, cardboard, glass, heavy paper and plastic foam surfaces are suitable for découpage. A variety of items are available at craft, hardware, and garden stores. Découpage is also a great way to revive and recycle an old suitcase, clay flowerpot, or wooden item.

Be certain surface is clean, smooth, and dry. Sand wood, terra-cotta, or tin surfaces. Base-coat in a coordinating or contrasting color unless you are covering the entire surface with prints. If the surface is to be completely covered with prints, base-coating is not required.

To create a background for prints, base-coat with a coordinating or contrasting color of acrylic craft paint. Individual project instructions include a wide variety of ideas for surfaces to use and backgrounds to create.

Applying the Base Coat

Using a flat or sponge brush and acrylic craft paint, apply base coat by brushing paint with the grain of the wood. Let dry. Sand surface with 220-grit sandpaper, sanding with the grain of the wood. Using a tack cloth, wipe away the excess dust.

Apply a second coat of base color. Let dry. If a third coat of paint is needed, sand and wipe away dust as before. Sanding between coats of paint smooths raised wood grain and gives the surface better tooth for the next coat of paint.

Sanding

Wood, terra-cotta, and tin items should be sanded with 220-grit sandpaper to smooth surfaces. On wooden surfaces, sand with the grain of the wood. Remove dust with tack cloth.

Preparing Prints for Découpage

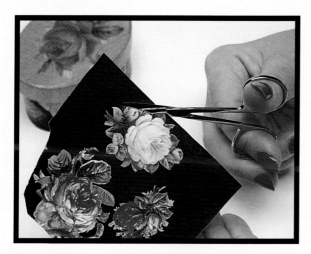

Cutting

Use small, sharp scissors such as embroidery, cuticle, or découpage scissors for cutting out designs. Cut away any inside areas you wish to remove, first by piercing the paper with the point of the scissors and cutting from the underside, then cut around the outer edge of the motif. Hold scissors stationary while you move and turn the print into the scissors for a smoother edge. If you are covering the entire surface, use a metal ruler or straightedge and a craft knife to ensure straight, smooth cuts.

Tearing

Tearing the edges of a print can create textural interest and add a handcrafted look. Tear in a downward direction to create a beveled edge for better adhesion. Aim for an uneven, irregular look.

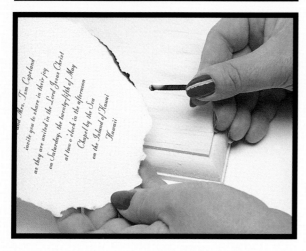

Burning

Burn the edges of a print for a rustic look. Use a match or candle flame to light the edges of the print and, just as the paper begins to burn, blow out the flame. Work one small area at a time, being cautious of the flame at all times. Remove excess charred paper, leaving an uneven brown edge.

Applying Prints

To cover an entire surface, measure, mark, and cut paper or fabric to fit area exactly. Use the object (such as a box lid) as a pattern, or measure the area and mark the paper or fabric before cutting. Use a straightedge and a craft knife to cut straight lines. Apply the print to the surface by following the instructions below and aligning the edges.

To cover corners, miter the print as if wrapping a package, creasing the paper to mark the edges of the surface. Cut away the excess paper at the creases, allowing the cut edges to butt together at the corner.

2 Position print on surface. Press with fingers to work out air bubbles. Be certain edges are adhered well.

1 Place cut-out print face down on waxed paper. Apply découpage finish to back of print.

3 Allow print to set up for a few minutes. Clean up area around print with damp paper towel or sponge. Let dry.

4 Using flat brush or sponge brush, apply découpage finish to entire project. Let dry on level surface. Sand between coats with 400-grit sandpaper. Apply second coat of découpage finish. Let dry overnight.

5 Optional: Two coats are sufficient to properly submerge and protect prints, but more coats may be applied. More thin coats are better than fewer thick ones. If you wish to have deeply submerged prints, apply four to six more coats of découpage finish.

6 Optional: For a satin-smooth look, wet 400-grit sandpaper and sand surface until finish is flat and smooth. Wipe dry. Polish surface with #0000 steel wool. Wipe. Your piece will have a lustrous matte finish. If you want a shiny finish, spray with a high-gloss acrylic sealer.

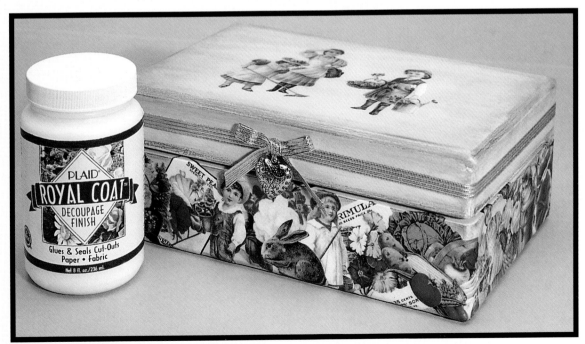

Special Surface Treatments

Painted surface treatments such as sponging, brushed textures, and marbleizing can add interest and texture to découpage. Other options for surface treatments include stenciling and crackling.

Use stenciling to create a background for découpage, as was done for the Stenciled Wine Cabinet on page 46, or to thematically link two objects, like the stenciled border on the Palm Tree Plate on page 51 that coordinates with the print découpaged on the Leopard Box, also on page 51. Choose from the wide variety of precut stencils and stencil paints available to create interesting backgrounds and borders for découpage prints.

To create the look of age and wear, add a crackled finish over or under découpage. The Crackled Fern Chest on pages 48–49 shows how effective crackling can be on top of your découpaged prints.

Antiquing

There are several ways to create an aged look.

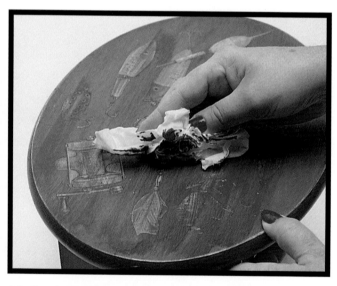

Method 1 One easy way is to use an antique-colored découpage finish to adhere your prints and finish the surface.

Method 2 Use an antiquing medium. First adhere prints, and then apply a coat of découpage finish. Let dry. Brush antiquing medium over surface and wipe away excess with a soft cloth. Let dry and apply additional coats of découpage finish to seal.

Method 3 Make an antiquing glaze with any paint color by mixing one part acrylic craft paint with three parts glazing medium. Brush mixture on surface, let dry, and apply additional coats of découpage finish to seal.

Reverse Découpaging

Reverse découpage involves applying prints to the back of a clear surface so print shows through front.

1 Cut out print. Apply découpage finish to print front. Press print, face down, onto back of clear plate. Smooth with fingers. Use damp paper towel to remove excess découpage finish from plate. Let dry.

2 To create background, paint backs of plate and print with acrylic paint. Let dry. Apply coat of découpage finish over paint to seal.

Découpaging on Fabric

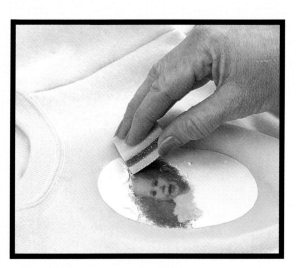

1 Trim photocopied photograph or print and place face up on waxed paper. Using sponge or sponge brush, apply photograph transfer medium onto front of photocopy. Note: The coat should be as thick as a dime, about 1/16". You will not be able to see the picture clearly.

2 While medium is wet, position photocopy face down on fabric. Lightly press paper to fabric, smoothing out wrinkles. Run finger around edge to seal. Using damp cloth, blot away excess. Let dry flat for 48 hours.

3 Place wet sponge on print to wet paper backing. Wait until paper looks saturated. Remove sponge and squeeze out water. Using damp sponge, rub off all visible paper. Let dry.

Découpaging on Candles

1 Cut out motifs from paper napkin. Separate and discard inner layers. Apply découpage finish to surface of candle. Press napkin print over surface, smoothing with fingers.

2 While print is wet, brush additional coat of découpage finish over entire candle to seal. Let dry.

Special Tips & Techniques

Sponging Background

Sponging creates an interesting background for découpage. First, base-coat the project. Let dry. Wet a sea or cellulose sponge; squeeze out excess water. Dip sponge into paint on a palette. Blot on a paper towel to remove excess. Press sponge on the project, then lift. Repeat, turning sponge a bit each time.

Adding 3-D Accents

Dimensional items like buttons, charms, braid, and ribbon can be added to découpage designs before or after the finish coats are applied. Adhere lightweight accents with a white craft glue; for heavier items, use hot glue.

Stenciling

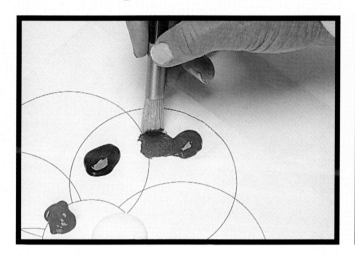

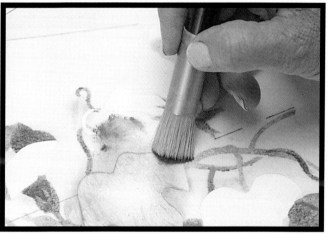

1 Squeeze dime-sized amount of acrylic craft paint or stencil gel onto palette. Hold stencil brush perpendicular to palette and pull out small amount of paint. Twist brush to concentrate most of paint in center of brush.

3 Swirl paint onto uncut portion of stencil to determine right amount of paint. Bring paint into cut-out area with light pouncing or circular stroke, keeping brush perpendicular to surface. Use more pressure to shade outside edges or for opaque print.

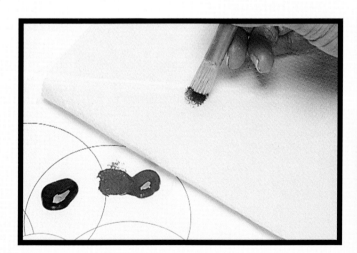

2 Swirl brush on paper towel to remove most of paint. Note: Stenciling is a dry-brushing technique; therefore, most mistakes are made by having too much paint on the brush.

Completed stenciled project.

Stamping

1 Load stamp with one color.

Note: If using a second color, add new paint color with a separate brush.

3 Release handle and gently press on back of stamp, pressing first in center of design, then on edges. Note: Use fingers, not heel of hand, for consistent pressure in all areas.

2 Hold loaded stamp by handle or side and position onto surface. Press firmly.

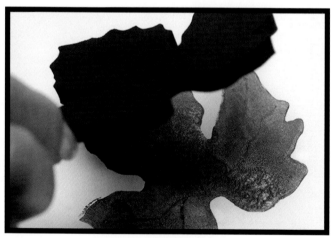

4 Lift stamp straight up off surface.

Cleaning Brushes

Brush Care & Cleanup

Brushes must be properly cleaned. When you buy a good-quality brush, it has sizing in it to hold the bristles in place. Before painting, remove the sizing by gently rubbing the bristles in your fingers. Then, thoroughly clean the brush with water. After completing the painted design, wash the brush, being careful not to abrade or abuse the bristles. Work the bristles back and forth with a brush cleaner. When the paint pigment is removed from the brush, leave the cleaner in the brush and shape with your fingers. Wrap bristles with rubber band when storing. Store brush flat or with bristles up—never store a brush with bristles down or bent. Rinse the brush before using it to paint.

2 Rub bristles on the scrubber that is attached to lid of brush cleaner. Work cleaner into lather and continue rubbing brush on scrubber while rinsing it under tap.

1 Dip tips of bristles into brush cleaner. Activate cleaner by dipping brush in water.

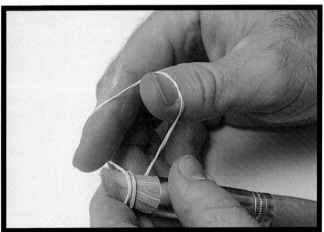

3 Remove excess water from bristles. Place rubber band around bristles. Let brush dry on its side.

Projects

Découpaging Memorabilia

Collections of tickets from special events, travel postcards, or other printed collections make wonderful designs to use for découpage. If you do not wish to use your precious memorabilia pieces, simply have them photocopied. The prints used in the projects shown here have all been photocopied on a color copier.

Traveler's Hatbox

Pictured on page 25

Designed by
Kathi Malarchuk Bailey

GATHER THESE SUPPLIES

Surface:
Papier-maché hatbox

Prints:
Color photocopies of travel stickers and postcards

Other Supplies:
Acrylic craft paints:
  Asphaltum
  Teddy Bear Tan
Chamois mitt
Découpage finish
Glazing medium
Sponge brushes

INSTRUCTIONS

Prepare Surface:
1. Refer to Preparing Surfaces on page 14. Prepare hatbox.

2. Using sponge brush, base-coat hatbox with two coats Teddy Bear Tan. Let dry.

Paint:
1. Mix Asphaltum and glazing medium (1:3). Using sponge brush, cover hatbox with Asphaltum glazing mixture.

2. While glaze is still wet, pounce damp chamois mitt over hatbox, removing some glaze and creating texture. Let dry overnight.

Prepare & Adhere Prints:
1. Refer to Preparing Prints for Découpage on page 15. Cut out travel stickers and postcards.

2. Refer to Applying Prints on pages 16–17. Using sponge brush, adhere cutouts onto hatbox with découpage finish. Let dry.

Finish:
1. Cover hatbox with two coats découpage finish to seal. Let dry.

Traveler's Hatbox

Instructions begin
on page 24

Violet Lamp

Designed by
Kathi Malarchuk Bailey

GATHER THESE SUPPLIES

Surface:
Glass or ceramic lamp

Prints:
Violet print greeting cards,
wrapping paper, or stationery

Other Supplies:
Acrylic craft paint:
  Bluebell
Découpage finish
Glazing medium
Sea sponge
Sponge brushes
White spray paint

INSTRUCTIONS

Prepare Surface:
1. Refer to Preparing Surfaces on page 14. Prepare lamp base.

2. Spray base with two coats White. Let dry.

Paint:
1. Refer to Sponging Background on page 20. Mix Bluebell and glazing medium (1:3). Using damp sponge, lightly sponge entire base with Bluebell glazing mixture. Let dry.

Prepare & Adhere Prints:
1. Refer to Preparing Prints for Découpage on page 15. Cut out violet motifs.

2. Refer to Applying Prints on pages 16–17. Using sponge brush, adhere cutouts onto base with découpage finish. Let dry.

Finish:
1. Cover base with two coats découpage finish to seal. Let dry.

Violet Drop-leaf Table

Designed by
Kathi Malarchuk Bailey

GATHER THESE SUPPLIES

Surface:
Unfinished wooden drop-leaf table

Prints:
Violet print greeting cards, wrapping paper, or stationery

Other Supplies:
Acrylic craft paints:
  Black
  Deep Purple
  Ivy Green
  Leaf Green
Brushes:
  #1 Round
  #6 Flat
  Sponge(s)
Crackle medium
Découpage finish
Latex paints:
  Blue
  Purple
  White
Sandpaper, #600 fine-grit
Stamping blocks:
  Little Garden Flowers

Continued on page 28

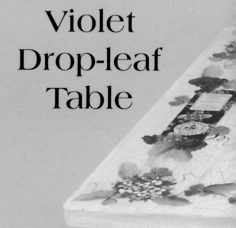

Violet Drop-leaf Table

Violet
Lamp

Continued from page 26

INSTRUCTIONS

Prepare Surface:
1. Refer to Preparing Surfaces on page 14. Prepare table.

Paint:
1. Using sponge brush, base-coat tabletop with two coats Blue, sanding between coats.

2. Base-coat table legs and lip with two coats Purple, sanding between coats. Let dry.

3. Using sponge brush, cover tabletop with crackle medium, following manufacturer's instructions. Let dry.

4. Using sponge brush, topcoat tabletop with White. Let dry.

Note: As paint dries it will begin to crackle.

5. Using sponge brush, cover tabletop with one coat découpage finish. Let dry.

Prepare & Adhere Prints:
1. Refer to Preparing Prints for Découpage on page 15. Cut out violet motifs.

2. Refer to Applying Prints on pages 16–17. Using sponge brush, adhere cutouts onto tabletop with découpage finish. Let dry.

Stamp:
1. Refer to Stamping on page 22. Using #6 flat brush, load leaves stamping blocks with Ivy Green and Leaf Green. Stamp tabletop.

2. Load small flower petals with Deep Purple and Black. Stamp tabletop.

3. Using round brush, add stems with Ivy Green. Let dry.

Finish:
1. Using sponge brush, cover entire table with two coats découpage finish to seal. Let dry.

Theatre Memories Table

Pictured on page 29

Designed by
Kathi Malarchuk Bailey

GATHER THESE SUPPLIES

Surface:
Unfinished wooden pedestal table, round

Prints:
Color photocopies of playbill covers and ticket stubs

Other Supplies:
Acrylic craft paints:
　Dove Gray
　Licorice
　Pure Gold
Brushes:
　#4 Flat
　Sponge(s)
Découpage finish
Glazing medium
Marbleizing feather
Sandpaper, #600 fine-grit
Sea sponge
White latex paint

INSTRUCTIONS

Prepare Surface:
1. Refer to Preparing Surfaces on page 14. Prepare table.

2. Using sponge brush, base-coat table with two coats White, sanding between coats. Let dry.

Paint:
1. Refer to Sponging Background on page 20. Mix Dove Gray and glazing medium (1:3). Using damp sponge, sponge drifts on table with Dove Gray glazing mixture. Let some white show through.

2. Mix Licorice and glazing medium (1:3). Sponge table with Licorice glazing mixture. Let lighter background show through.

3. Using feather, lightly pull veins on tabletop with Licorice glazing mixture. Repeat veining with Pure Gold.

4. Using sponge, lightly sponge over veins to mute.

5. Using sponge brush, paint trim with Pure Gold. Paint legs with Licorice. Let dry.

Prepare & Adhere Prints:
1. Refer to Preparing Prints for Découpage on page 15. Cut out playbill covers and ticket stubs.

2. Refer to Applying Prints on pages 16–17. Using sponge brush, adhere cutouts onto tabletop with découpage finish. Let dry.

3. Using flat brush, paint shadows around tickets and playbills with Licorice glazing mixture. Let dry.

Finish:
1. Using sponge brush, cover table with two coats découpage finish to seal. Let dry.

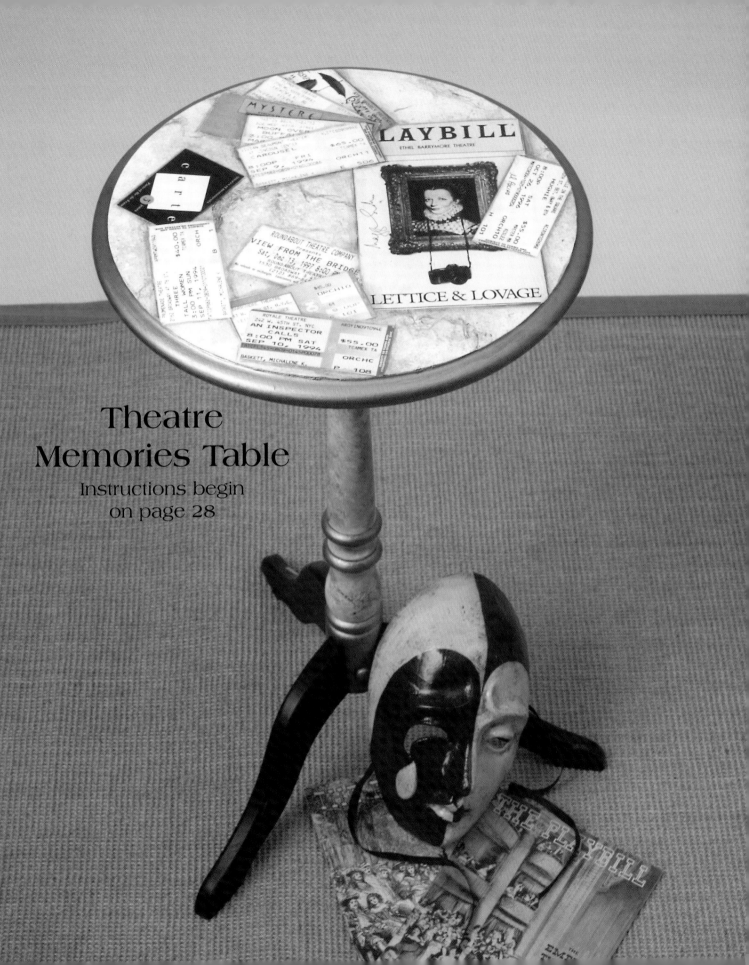

Theatre
Memories Table
Instructions begin
on page 28

Galvanized Party Pail

*Designed by
Ann Barnes*

GATHER THESE SUPPLIES

Surface:
Galvanized bucket, oblong

Prints:
Color prints of champagne
   glasses

Other Supplies:
Acrylic craft paints:
   Burnt Umber
   Licorice
Brushes:
   #4 Flat
   Sponge(s)
Découpage finish
Glazing medium
Gold star garland, 9'

INSTRUCTIONS

Prepare Surface:
1. Refer to Preparing Surfaces on page 14. Prepare
bucket.

2. Using sponge brush,
highlight raised areas of
bucket with Licorice.
Let dry.

Prepare & Adhere Prints:
1. Refer to Preparing Prints
for Découpage on page 15.
Cut out champagne glass
motifs.

2. Refer to Applying Prints
on pages 16–17. Using
sponge brush, adhere cut-
outs onto bucket with
découpage finish. Let dry.
Continued on page 32

Galvanized
Party Pail

Wine
Label Tray
Instructions begin
on page 32

Continued from page 30

Antique:
1. Refer to Antiquing on page 18. Mix Burnt Umber with glazing medium (1:3). Using flat brush, antique cutouts with Burnt Umber mixture. Let dry.

Finish:
1. Tie star garland around top of bucket.

Wine Label Tray

Pictured on pages 30–31

Designed by
Kathi Malarchuk Bailey

GATHER THESE SUPPLIES

Surface:
Papier-maché tray, 14" square

Prints:
Labels from wine bottles

Other Supplies:
Acrylic craft paints:
  Licorice
  Pure Gold
  Summer Sky
  Tartan Green
  Wicker White
Cellulose sponge
Découpage finish
Glazing medium
Marbleizing feather
Metallic gold wax finish
Sandpaper, #600 fine-grit
Soft cloth
Sponge brushes

INSTRUCTIONS

Prepare Surface:
1. Refer to Preparing Surfaces on page 14. Prepare tray.

2. Using sponge brush, basecoat entire tray with two coats Licorice, sanding between coats. Let dry.

Paint:
1. Refer to Sponging Background on page 20. Mix Tartan Green and glazing medium (1:3). Using damp sponge, sponge drifts on tray with Tartan Green glazing mixture Let black show through.

2. While paint is still wet, repeat procedure with mixture Summer Sky and glazing medium (1:3).

3. Randomly highlight with mixture of Wicker White and glazing medium (1:3).

4. Using feather, lightly pull veins on tabletop with Wicker White glazing mixture.

5. Randomly highlight with mixture of Pure Gold and glazing medium (1:3).

6. Lightly pull veins on tabletop with Pure Gold glazing mixture.

7. Using sponge, lightly sponge over portions of veins to mute.

Prepare & Adhere Prints:
1. Refer to Preparing Prints for Découpage on page 15. Cut out wine labels.

2. Refer to Applying Prints on pages 16–17. Using sponge brush, adhere cutouts onto tray with découpage finish. Let dry.

Finish:
1. Using soft cloth, rub tray edges with metallic gold wax finish, following manufacturer's instructions.

2. Using sponge brush, cover entire tray with two coats découpage finish to seal. Let dry.

A black-and-white print can be elegant, bold, simple, or understated. It can create an antique look or a contemporary one. Copy or clip prints from art books, computer images, gift wrap, old books magazines, or wallpaper. Use a photocopier to size the print to fit the surface and create multiples. For interesting shades of gray, copy a black-and-white image on a color copier. You can copy onto textured or colored papers.

Tinting:
Method 1: Black-and-white prints can be tinted using acrylic craft paints mixed with glazing medium (1:1).

Method 2: Using colored pencils is an easy way to add soft color to black-and-white prints.

Classic Urns Wastebasket

Pictured on page 35

Designed by
Lauren Powell

GATHER THESE SUPPLIES

Surface:
Wooden wastebasket

Print:
Urn print wallpaper

Other Supplies:
Acrylic craft paint:
  Taffy
Brown antiquing medium
Crackle medium
Découpage finish
Matte varnish
Sea sponge
Sponge brushes

INSTRUCTIONS

Prepare Surface:
1. Refer to Preparing Surfaces on page 14. Prepare wastebasket.

2. Using sponge brush, base-coat wastebasket with Taffy. Let dry.

Prepare & Adhere Prints:
1. Refer to Preparing Prints for Découpage on page 15. Cut out urn motifs from wallpaper.

2. Refer to Applying Prints on pages 16–17. Using sponge brush, adhere cutouts onto wastebasket with découpage finish. Let dry.

Finish:
1. Using sponge, cover entire wastebasket with crackle medium. Let dry.

2. Using sponge brush, thickly cover wastebasket with varnish, without overlapping strokes. Let dry.

Note: As varnish dries it will begin to crackle.

3. Using sponge, rub antiquing medium into cracks. Let dry.

Poppy Tissue Cover

Pictured on page 35

Designed by
Ann Barnes

GATHER THESE SUPPLIES

Surface:
Unfinished wooden tissue box, square

Prints:
Photocopies of black-and-white botanical poppy print, tinted with colored pencils (4)

Other Supplies:
Acrylic craft paints:
  Brilliant Ultramarine
  Pure Gold
  Tapioca
Crackle medium
Découpage finish
Metallic gold wax finish
Sandpaper, #600 fine-grit
Sea sponge
Soft cloth
Sponge brushes
Continued on page 34

Continued from page 33

INSTRUCTIONS

Prepare Surface:
1. Refer to Preparing Surfaces on page 14. Prepare tissue box.

Paint:
1. Using sponge brush, base-coat tissue box with two coats Brilliant Ultramarine, sanding between coats. Let dry.

2. Lightly brush on one coat Pure Gold. Let dry.

3. Using sponge, cover entire box with crackle medium. Let dry.

4. Using sponge brush, top-coat box with Tapioca. Let dry.

5. Using sponge brush, cover box with one coat découpage finish. Let dry.

Prepare & Adhere Prints:
1. Refer to Preparing Prints for Découpage on page 15. Cut out poppy motifs.

2. Refer to Applying Prints on pages 16–17. Using sponge brush, adhere cutouts onto box with découpage finish. Let dry.

Finish:
1. Using sponge brush, cover entire box with two coats découpage finish. Let dry.

2. Using soft cloth, rub box edges with metallic gold wax finish, following manufacturer's instructions.

Triptych Clock

Pictured on page 35

Designed by
Lauren Powell

GATHER THESE SUPPLIES

Surface:
Large wooden cathedral triptych

Prints:
Photocopies of black-and-white cathedral interiors and architectural accents

Other Supplies:
Acrylic craft paints:
    Asphaltum
    Black
Black spray paint
Brushes:
    #4 Flat
    Sponge(s)
Clock movement, ⅜"
Craft knife
Découpage finish
Drill & drill bit
Glazing medium
Metallic gold wax finish
Matte acrylic spray sealer
Soft cloth

INSTRUCTIONS

Prepare Surface:
1. Refer to Preparing Surfaces on page 14. Prepare panels.

2. Using sponge brush, base-coat triptych with Black. Let dry.

3. Spray clock movement with Black.

Prepare & Adhere Prints:
1. Refer to Preparing Prints for Découpage on page 15. Cut out cathedral motifs to fit triptych.

2. Refer to Applying Prints on pages 16–17. Using sponge brush, adhere cutouts onto triptych with découpage finish, lining up edges. Let dry.

3. Using craft knife, trim excess paper around hinges.

4. Cover entire surface with one coat découpage finish. Let dry.

Antique:
1. Refer to Antiquing on page 18. Mix Asphaltum and glazing medium (1:3). Using flat brush, antique cutouts with Asphaltum mixture. Let dry.

2. Using soft cloth, rub edges and over prints with metallic gold wax finish, following manufacturer's instructions.

Finish:
1. Spray triptych with matte acrylic sealer.

2. Drill hole in center screen for clock movement. Assemble clock.

Triptych Clock
Instructions begin on page 34

Classic Urns Wastebasket
Instructions begin on page 33

Poppy Tissue Cover
Instructions begin on page 33

Floral Woodgrain Box

Instructions begin on page 38

Floral Woodgrain Box

Pictured on pages 36–37

Designed by
Julie Watkins Schreiner

GATHER THESE SUPPLIES

Surface:
Stained wooden box, 12" long

Print:
Woodgrain print wrapping
   paper

Other Supplies:
Acrylic craft paint:
   Pure Gold
Brushes:
   ½" Flat
   ¼" Stencil
Découpage finish
Stencils:
   Label
   Picture Frame Corners

INSTRUCTIONS

Prepare Surface:
1. Refer to Preparing Surfaces on page 14. Prepare box.

Prepare & Adhere Prints:
1. Refer to Preparing Prints for Découpage on page 15. Tear wrapping paper 1½" to 2" smaller than box lid.

2. Cut out desired motifs from wrapping paper for front and sides of box.

3. Refer to Applying Prints on pages 16–17. Using flat brush, adhere cutouts onto box with découpage finish. Let dry.

Finish:
1. Refer to Stenciling on page 21. Using stencil brush, stencil corner motifs and label motif onto box with Pure Gold. Let dry.

2. Using flat brush, cover box with two coats découpage finish. Let dry.

Compact Disc Box

Pictured on page 39

Designed by
Ann Barnes

GATHER THESE SUPPLIES

Surface:
Wooden compact disc box

Print:
Sheet music

Other Supplies:
Acrylic craft paint:
   Burnt Umber
Black spray paint
Découpage finish
Glazing medium
Sponge brushes

INSTRUCTIONS

Prepare Surface:
1. Refer to Preparing Surfaces on page 14. Prepare box.

2. Spray entire box with Black.

Prepare & Adhere Prints:
1. Refer to Preparing Prints for Découpage on page 15. Cut sheet music to fit box.

2. Refer to Applying Prints on pages 16–17. Using sponge brush, adhere cutouts onto box with découpage finish.

Finish:
1. Refer to Antiquing on page 18. Mix Burnt Umber and glazing medium (1:3). Using sponge brush, antique box with Burnt Umber mixture. Let dry.

2. Using sponge brush, cover box with two coats découpage finish. Let dry.

Compact
Disc
Box

Instructions
begin on
page 38

Three Hearts Plaque

Instructions begin on page 42

Three Hearts Plaque

Pictured on pages 40–41

Designed by
Paula Joerling

GATHER THESE SUPPLIES

Surface:
Plastic foam sheet,
½" x 15" x 18"

Print:
Newspaper

Other Supplies:
Acrylic craft paints:
  Blue Ribbon
  Lemon Custard
  Lipstick Red
  Purple Passion
Brushes:
  1" Flat
  #6 Flat
  Sponge
Découpage finish
Heavy books
Hot-glue gun & glue sticks
Matte knife
Newsprint paper
Picture hanger
Sandpaper, #600 fine-grit
Straightedge
Thick white craft glue
Waxed paper

INSTRUCTIONS

Make Plaque:
1. Refer to Diagrams 1 & 2. Using straightedge and matte knife, cut out two pieces from foam.

2. Refer to Tracing & Transferring Patterns on page 13. Using Heart Pattern on page 43, transfer three hearts onto remaining foam.

3. Using matte knife cut out hearts.

4. Lightly sand edges of hearts to remove burrs.

Prepare Surface:
1. Refer to Preparing Surfaces on page 14. Prepare plaque.

2. Using #6 flat brush, lightly coat all surfaces with découpage finish. Let dry.

Prepare & Adhere Prints:
1. Refer to Preparing Prints for Découpage on page 15. Tear newspaper into pieces.

Diagram 1

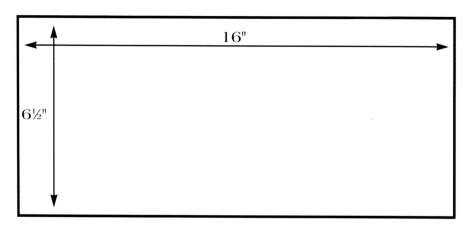

Diagram 2

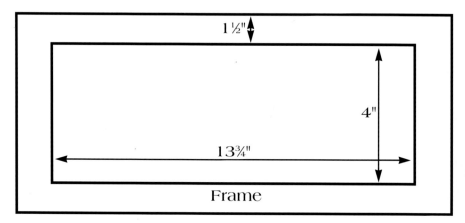

Frame

2. Refer to Applying Prints on pages 16–17. Adhere torn newspaper onto front and sides of hearts and frame piece.

Paint:

1. Mix Lemon Custard and découpage finish (1:3). Using 1" flat brush, paint background with Lemon Custard découpage mixture. Apply sheer coats, using more paint in some areas to create a mottled look.

2. Mix Purple Passion and découpage finish (1:3). Using #6 flat brush, paint first heart trim and Xs with Purple Passion découpage mixture.

3. Mix Lipstick Red with découpage finish (1:3). Using 1" flat brush, paint second heart with Lipstick Red découpage mixture.

4. Using #6 brush, paint red border with Lipstick Red.

5. Mix Blue Ribbon and découpage finish (1:3). Using 1" flat brush, paint third heart with Blue Ribbon découpage mixture.

6. Using #6 brush, paint blue Os with Blue Ribbon.

7. Paint Xs and Os and 'Love' on frame with Lipstick Red. Let dry.

Finish:

1. Adhere back of frame onto background with craft glue.

2. Cover frame with waxed paper and lay heavy books on top to assure an even bond. Let dry.

3. Remove books and waxed paper. Using sponge brush, adhere more torn newspaper onto outside frame edges with découpage finish. Let newspaper wrap around to back about ½". Let dry.

4. Center and adhere hearts onto background with craft glue.

5. Cover frame with waxed paper and lay heavy books on top to assure an even bond. Let dry.

6. Adhere newsprint paper onto plaque back.

7. Using hot-glue gun, adhere picture hanger onto back.

Heart Pattern

Pattern is actual size

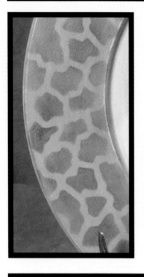

Postcards, labels, wrapping paper, napkins, stationery, or even a puzzle can add design and dimension to a project.

Projects can be further enhanced by using special treatments such as stenciling, sponging, crackling, antiquing, and stamping.

Pastoral Clock

Pictured on page 45

Designed by
Kathi Malarchuk Bailey

GATHER THESE SUPPLIES

Surface:
Unfinished wooden clock with
    bezel, 9½" tall

Print:
Landscape postcard or
    greeting card

Other Supplies:
Acrylic craft paints:
    Burnt Umber
    Coastal Blue
    Fresh Foliage
    Light Periwinkle
    Old Ivy
    Wicker White
Brushes:
    ¼" Stencil
    Sponge(s)
Découpage finish
Sandpaper, #600 fine-grit
Sea sponge

INSTRUCTIONS

Prepare Surface:
1. Refer to Preparing Surfaces on page 14. Prepare clock.

2. Using sponge brush, base-coat entire clock with two coats Wicker White, sanding between coats. Let dry.

3. Paint clock trim with Light Periwinkle.

Paint:
1. Refer to Sponging Background on page 20. Using damp sponge, lightly sponge top two-thirds of clock with Coastal Blue, creating sky area.

2. Sponge on small amount Light Periwinkle.

3. Using stencil brush, pounce with Wicker White to form clouds.

4. Sponge bottom one-third of clock with Fresh Foliage, creating ground.

5. Shade one-third of bottom with Burnt Umber and Old Ivy. Let dry two hours.

Prepare & Adhere Print:
1. Refer to Preparing Prints for Découpage on page 15. Cut out landscape motif.

2. Refer to Applying Prints on pages 16–17. Using sponge brush, adhere cutout onto clock with découpage finish. Let dry.

Finish:
1. Cover clock with two coats découpage finish to seal. Let dry.

Pastoral Clock

Instructions begin
on page 44

QUARTZ

TAIWAN

Stenciled Wine Cabinet

Instructions begin
on page 47

Stenciled Wine Cabinet

Pictured on page 46

Designed by
Kathi Malarchuk Bailey

GATHER THESE SUPPLIES

Surface:
Wooden cabinet

Prints:
Labels from wine bottles

Other Supplies:
Acrylic craft paint:
  Olive Green
Brushes:
  Sponge(s)
  Stencil(s)
Découpage finish
Latex paint:
  Light Green
Masking tape
Sandpaper, #600 fine-grit
Stencil:
  Grapes
Stencil gel paints:
  Deep Purple
  Fern
  Twig
  Wild Ivy

INSTRUCTIONS

Prepare Surface:
1. Refer to Preparing Surfaces on page 14. Prepare cabinet.

2. Using sponge brush, base-coat cabinet with two coats Light Green, sanding between coats. Let dry.

Stencil:
1. Refer to Stenciling on page 21. Using stencil brush, stencil grapes onto cabinet with Deep Purple and Fern.

2. Stencil leaves with Fern, Twig, and Wild Ivy.

Paint:
1. Using masking tape, mask-off top trim and door trim.

2. Using sponge brush, base-coat cabinet with two coats Olive Green, sanding between coats. Let dry.

Prepare & Adhere Prints:
1. Refer to Preparing Prints for Découpage on page 15. Cut out wine labels.

2. Refer to Applying Prints on pages 16–17. Using sponge brush, adhere cutouts onto cabinet with découpage finish. Let dry.

Finish:
1. Cover cabinet with two coats découpage finish to seal. Let dry.

Crackled Fern Chest

Pictured on pages 48–49

Designed by
Lauren Powell

GATHER THESE SUPPLIES

Surface:
Unfinished wooden box

Print:
Fern print wrapping paper

Other Supplies:
Acrylic craft paints:
  Basil Green
  Taffy
Brown antiquing medium
Brushes:
  Liner
  Sponge(s)
Crackle medium
Découpage finish
Matte varnish
Sea sponge

INSTRUCTIONS

Prepare Surface:
1. Refer to Preparing Surfaces on page 14. Prepare box.

2. Using sponge brush, base-coat box with Taffy. Let dry.

3. Using liner, outline frames on box to frame fern panels with Basil Green. Let dry.

Prepare & Adhere Prints:
1. Refer to Preparing Prints for Découpage on page 15. Cut out fern motifs from wrapping paper.

2. Refer to Applying Prints on pages 16–17. Using sponge brush, adhere cutouts onto box with découpage finish. Let dry.

Finish:
1. Using sponge brush, cover entire box with crackle medium, following manufacturer's instructions.

2. Using sponge brush, cover entire box with varnish. Let dry.

Note: As varnish dries it will begin to crackle.

3. Refer to Antiquing on page 18. Using sponge, rub cracks with antiquing medium. Let dry.

4. Cover chest with two coats découpage finish to seal. Let dry.

Crackled Fern Chest

Instructions begin on page 47

Palm Tree Plate

Pictured on page 51

Designed by
Lauren Powell

GATHER THESE SUPPLIES

Surface:
Wooden plate, 11½" dia.

Print:
Palm tree

Other Supplies:
Acrylic craft paints:
  Asphaltum
  Sunflower
  Yellow Ochre
Brushes:
  ½" Stencil
  Sponge
Découpage finish
Dry-brush stencil paint:
  Truffles Brown
Glazing medium
Stencil:
  Skins

INSTRUCTIONS

Prepare Surface:
1. Refer to Preparing Surfaces on page 14. Prepare plate.

2. Using sponge brush, base-coat plate center with Sunflower.

3. Base-coat rim and back with Yellow Ochre. Let dry.

Prepare & Adhere Print:
1. Refer to Preparing Prints for Découpage on page 15. Cut out palm tree motif.

2. Refer to Applying Prints on pages 16–17. Using sponge brush, adhere cutout onto plate center with découpage finish. Let dry.

3. Cover entire center area with one coat découpage finish. Let dry.

Antique:
1. Refer to Antiquing on page 18. Mix Asphaltum and glazing medium (1:3). Using sponge brush, antique cutout with Asphaltum mixture. Let dry.

Stencil:
1. Refer to Stenciling on page 21. Using stencil brush, stencil animal skin motif onto plate rim with Truffles Brown. Let dry.

Finish:
1. Using sponge brush, cover entire plate with découpage finish to seal. Let dry.

Leopard Box

Pictured on page 51

Designed by
Lauren Powell

GATHER THESE SUPPLIES

Surface:
Wooden trunk

Prints:
Leopard print stationery
Leopard-skin print paper
  napkin

Other Supplies:
Acrylic craft paint:
  Black
Acrylic gloss sealer spray
Decorative knob
Découpage finish
Sandpaper, #600 fine-grit
Sponge brushes

INSTRUCTIONS

Prepare Surface:
1. Refer to Preparing Surfaces on page 14. Prepare trunk.

2. Using sponge brush, base-coat sides and inside of box (but not the lid or bottom edge) with two coats Black. Let dry.

Prepare & Adhere Prints:
1. Refer to Preparing Prints for Découpage on page 15. Cut out leopard-skin napkin to fit box top. Separate and discard inner layers.

2. Refer to Applying Prints on pages 16–17. Using sponge brush, adhere cutout onto box top with découpage finish, lining up border on edges. Let dry.

3. Adhere napkin border onto box base.

4. Adhere leopard print onto front center of box.

5. Cover box with découpage finish. Let dry.

Finish:
1. Spray entire box with acrylic gloss sealer. Let dry.

2. Screw knob to top.

Palm Tree Plate

Instructions begin
on page 50

Leopard Box

Instructions begin
on page 50

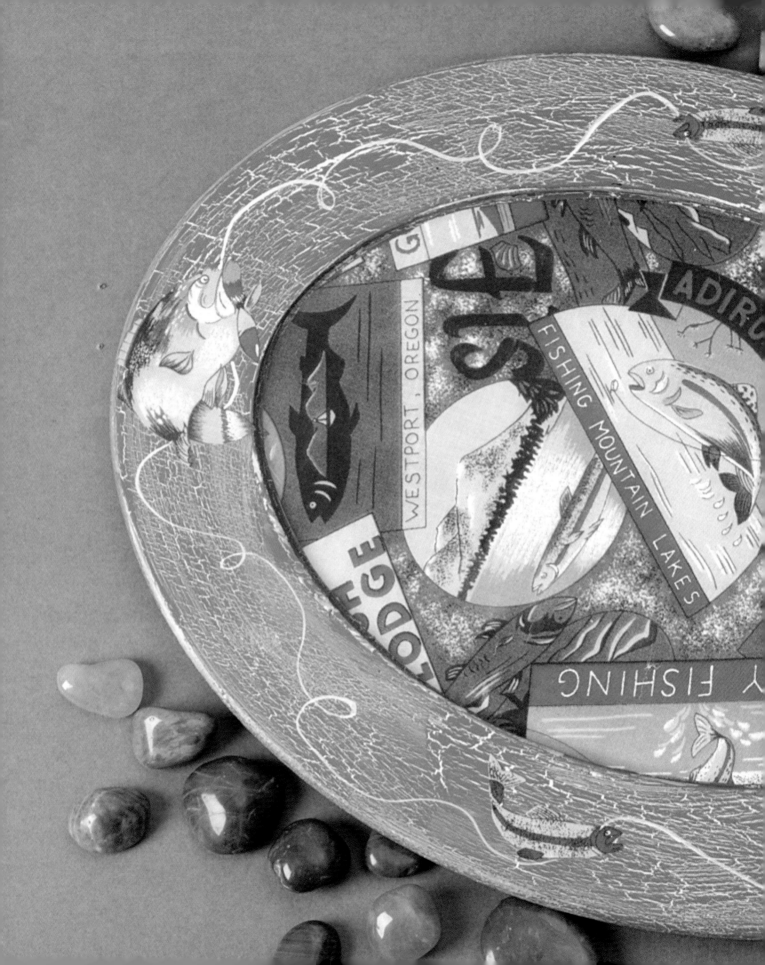

Fish Tray

Instructions begin on page 54

Fish Tray

Pictured on pages 52–53

Designed by
Kathi Malarchuk Bailey

GATHER THESE SUPPLIES

Surface:
Unfinished wooden tray, oval

Print:
Fish label fabric (⅓ yd)

Other Supplies:
Acrylic craft paints:
  Teal Green
  Warm White
Brushes:
  Liner
  Sponge(s)
Crackle medium
Découpage finish
Sandpaper, #600 fine-grit

INSTRUCTIONS

Prepare Surface:
1. Refer to Preparing Surfaces on page 14. Prepare tray.

2. Using sponge brush, base-coat tray with two coats Warm White, sanding between coats. Let dry.

3. Using sponge brush, cover plate lip with crackle medium, following manufacturer's instructions. Let dry.

4. Using sponge brush, topcoat plate with Teal Green. Let dry.

Note: As paint dries it will begin to crackle.

Prepare & Adhere Prints:
1. Refer to Preparing Prints for Découpage on page 15. Cut out fabric fish labels and individual fish motifs.

2. Refer to Applying Prints on pages 16–17. Using sponge brush, adhere cutouts onto tray with découpage finish. Let dry.

Finish:
1. Using liner, paint curling lines between fish on plate lip with Warm White.

2. Using sponge brush, cover plate with two coats découpage finish to seal. Let dry.

Puzzle-top Box

Pictured on page 55

Designed by
Kathi Malarchuk Bailey

GATHER THESE SUPPLIES

Surface:
Unfinished wooden box, 9" x 12"

Print:
Puzzle, 8" x 10"

Other Supplies:
Acrylic craft paint:
  Antique Gold
Cellulose sponge
Craft knife
Foil kit
Gold cording (1⅓ yd.)
Hot-glue gun & glue sticks
Puzzle saver
Ruler
Sandpaper, #600 fine-grit
Sponge brushes

INSTRUCTIONS

Prepare Surface:
1. Refer to Preparing Surfaces on page 14. Prepare box.

2. Using sponge brush, base-coat box with two coats Antique Gold, sanding between coats. Let dry 2–3 hours.

3. Refer to Applying Prints on pages 16–17. Using sponge, sponge foil adhesive over entire box so sponge texture shows and surface is not completely covered. Let adhesive dry until clear.

4. Apply gold foil to adhesive on box, following manufacturer's instructions.

Prepare & Adhere Print:
1. Refer to Preparing Prints for Découpage on page 15. Complete puzzle.

2. Using sponge brush, cover back of puzzle with one coat puzzle saver. Let dry 30 minutes.

3. Using craft knife and ruler, trim puzzle to fit in center of box top.

4. Using sponge brush, cover puzzle back with another coat puzzle saver. Position puzzle on box and press in place. Let dry 30 minutes.

Finish:
1. Cover puzzle and entire box with two coats puzzle saver. Let dry between coats.

2. Using hot-glue gun, adhere gold cord around puzzle edge.

3. Tie a knot at right center of gold cording. Tie a knot 1½" from ends and unravel ends to create tassel.

Puzzle-top Box
Instructions begin
on page 54

Photographs are not just for putting in albums. You can display pictures of your loved ones and friends by découpaging them to the surface of almost any object. To preserve the original photograph, be certain to use a color copy for your projects.

Découpage is a wonderful way to preserve invitations and wedding, graduation, and birth announcements. Choose enhancements, such as additional découpage or decorative painting, appropriate to the occasion commemorated.

Box Frame

Pictured on page 57

Designed by
Ann Barnes

GATHER THESE SUPPLIES

Surface:
Picture frame with printed
border, 4" x 6"

Print:
Color photocopy of
photograph

Other Supplies:
Découpage finish
Sponge brush

INSTRUCTIONS

Prepare Surface:
1. Refer to Preparing Surfaces on page 14. Prepare frame.

Prepare & Adhere Print:
1. Refer to Preparing Prints for Découpage on page 15. Cut photocopy to fit frame opening.

2. Refer to Applying Prints on pages 16–17. Using sponge brush, adhere cutout onto frame with découpage finish. Let dry.

Finish:
1. Cover entire front of print with découpage finish to seal. Let dry.

Photograph Album

Pictured on page 57

Designed by
Ann Barnes

GATHER THESE SUPPLIES

Surface:
Photograph album with printed
frame border

Print:
Color photocopy of
photograph

Other Supplies:
Craft glue
Découpage finish
Gold braid
Sponge brush

INSTRUCTIONS

Prepare Surface:
1. Refer to Preparing Surfaces on page 14. Prepare album.

Prepare & Adhere Print:
1. Refer to Preparing Prints for Découpage on page 15. Cut photocopy to fit album frame.

2. Refer to Applying Prints on pages 16–17. Using sponge brush, adhere cutout onto album with découpage finish. Let dry.

Finish:
1. Cover entire front of print with découpage finish to seal. Let dry.

2. Adhere gold braid to album with craft glue, securing ends inside cover.

Photograph Album
Instructions begin on page 56

Box Frame
Instructions begin
on page 56

Photographs

Dog Frame

Pictured on page 59

Designed by
Susan Lowenthal

GATHER THESE SUPPLIES

Surface:
Wooden picture frame

Prints:
Color photocopies of dog
   photographs

Other Supplies:
Acrylic craft paint:
   Warm White
Découpage finish
High-gloss glaze spray
Sandpaper, #600 fine-grit
Sponge brush

INSTRUCTIONS

Prepare Surface:
1. Refer to Preparing Surfaces
on page 14. Prepare frame.

2. Using sponge brush, base-
coat frame with two coats
Warm White, sanding between
coats. Let dry.

Prepare & Adhere Prints:
1. Refer to Preparing Prints for
Découpage on page 15. Cut
out dog motifs.

2. Refer to Applying Prints on
pages 16–17. Using sponge
brush, adhere cutouts onto
frame with découpage finish.
Let dry.

3. Cover entire surface with
découpage finish. Let dry.

Finish:
1. Spray frame with several
coats high-gloss glaze.

Dog Plate

Pictured on page 59

Designed by
Susan Lowenthal

GATHER THESE SUPPLIES

Surface:
Clear glass plate, octagonal

Print:
Color photocopy of dog
   photograph

Other Supplies:
Acrylic craft paints:
   Copper
   Licorice
   Pure Gold
   Silver Sterling
Black permanent marker
Brayer
Brushes:
   1" Wash
   #4 Fan
   Sponge
Craft knife
Découpage finish
Gold glitter paint
Gold leafing pen
Gold paint pen
Paper towels
Rubbing alcohol
Ruler
Sea sponge
Spray fixative
Waxed paper

INSTRUCTIONS

Prepare Surface:
1. Refer to Preparing Surfaces
on page 14. Using rubbing
alcohol and paper towels,
clean plate. Let dry.

2. Refer to Reverse Découpaging on page 19. Using gold
leafing pen, outline inner and
outer edges of rim.

Prepare & Adhere Print:
1. Using black marker, black-
out photograph background.

2. Using gold paint pen, write
dog's name on print. Let dry.

3. Spray photograph with
fixative. Let dry.

4. Refer to Preparing Prints for
Découpage on page 15. Using
ruler and craft knife, cut out
photograph to fit inside plate.

5. Dip photograph briefly in
water. Place on waxed paper,
right side up.

6. Refer to Applying Prints on
pages 16–17. Using wash
brush, cover front of photograph and plate back with
découpage finish.

7. Place photograph face
down on plate back. Using
brayer, smooth. Using paper
towel, clean excess découpage finish from rim. Let dry
24 hours.

Paint:
1. Using fan brush tips, lightly
cover rim back with gold
glitter. Let dry.

2. Using sponge, sponge rim
back alternately with Copper,
Pure Gold, and Silver Sterling.
Let dry.

3. Using sponge brush, cover
plate back with Licorice.
Let dry.

Finish:
1. Using sponge brush, cover
plate with two to three coats
découpage finish to seal.
Let dry.

Dog Frame

Instructions begin on page 58

Dog Plate

Instructions begin on page 58

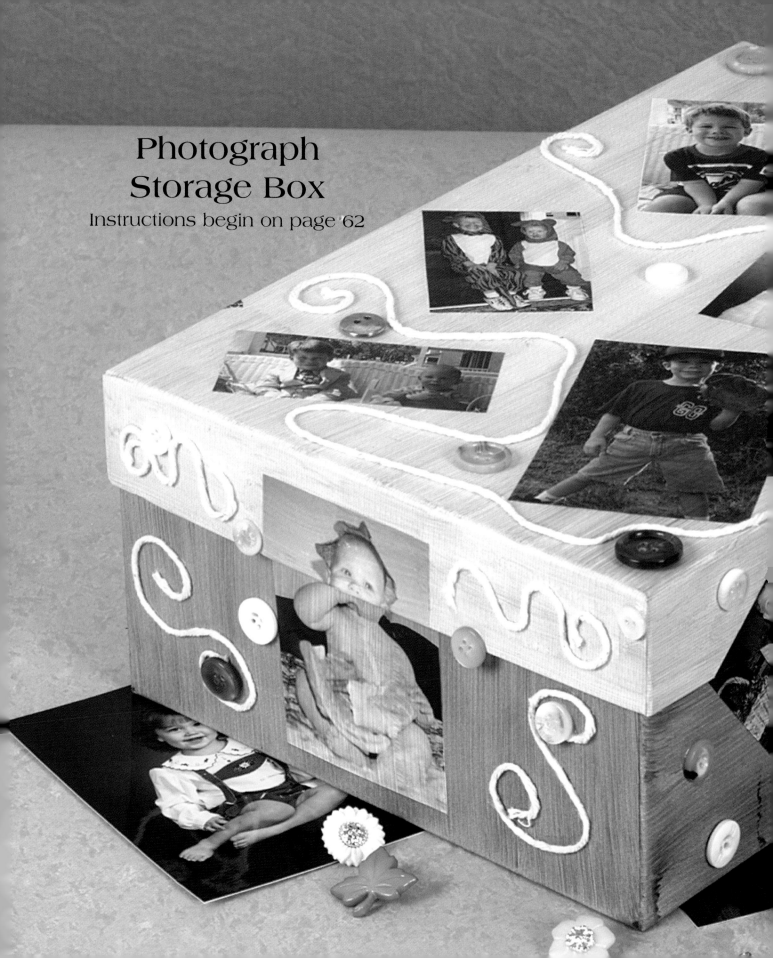

Photograph
Storage Box
Instructions begin on page 62

Photograph Storage Box

Pictured on pages 60–61

Designed by
Ann Barnes

GATHER THESE SUPPLIES

Surface:
Cardboard storage box

Prints:
Color photocopies of
  photographs

Other Supplies:
Acrylic craft paint:
  Burnt Umber
Assorted buttons (30–50)
Découpage finish
Glazing medium
Sponge brushes
Twine
White craft glue

INSTRUCTIONS

Prepare Surface:
1. Refer to Preparing Surfaces on page 14. Prepare box.

Prepare & Adhere Prints:
1. Refer to Preparing Prints for Découpage on page 15. Cut out photographs.

2. Refer to Applying Prints on pages 16–17. Using sponge brush, adhere cutouts onto box with découpage finish. Let dry.

Antique:
1. Refer to Antiquing on page 18. Mix Burnt Umber with glazing medium (1:3). Using sponge brush and Burnt Umber glazing mixture, antique box, including photographs. Let dry.

Finish:
1. Randomly adhere twine and buttons onto box with craft glue.

2. Using sponge brush, cover box with two coats découpage finish to seal. Let dry.

Bulletin Board

Pictured on page 63

Designed by
Julie Watkins Schreiner

GATHER THESE SUPPLIES

Surface:
Plastic foam sheet,
  ½" x 14" x 17"

Prints:
Photocopies of black-and-white
  photographs, cards, or
  memos (Reverse any copies
  with text.) (5)

Other Supplies:
Acrylic craft paint:
  Licorice
Burgundy fabric, 18" x 21"
Craft glue
Flat brush, ¼"-wide
Photograph transfer medium,
  clear
Poster board, 13½" x 16½"
Quilt batting, 14" x 17"

Ribbons:
  Coordinating print 2"-wide,
    18"
  Olive satin, ¼"-wide (4 yds)
Upholstery tacks (5)

INSTRUCTIONS

Prepare Surface:
1. Refer to Preparing Surfaces on page 14. Prepare foam.

Prepare & Adhere Prints:
1. Refer to Découpaging on Fabric on page 19. Transfer photocopies onto fabric within 14" x 17" area, with photograph transfer medium.

Paint:
1. Using flat brush, paint borders around each photograph with Licorice.

Finish:
1. Adhere batting onto back with craft glue.

2. Vertically wrap fabric around batting and foam. Adhere edges onto back.

3. Diagonally position satin ribbon pieces across fabric and adhere edges onto back.

4. Dip tips of upholstery tacks in glue and press into foam where ribbons intersect.

5. Fold 2" ribbon in half and glue ends onto center top back of foam for hanger.

6. Glue poster board securely onto back to cover all raw edges.

Bulletin Board
Instructions begin
on page 62

Memories of Mother Plate

Pictured on page 65

Designed by
Chris Adams, SCD

GATHER THESE SUPPLIES

Surface:
Wooden plate, 11½" octagonal

Prints:
Photocopy of black-and-white
   photograph
Prints of poem or other
   memorabilia

Other Supplies:
Acrylic craft paints:
   French Vanilla
   Inca Gold
   Pure Gold Metallic
Decorative-edged scissors
Découpage finish
Embellishments:
   Berries
   Brass heart
   Burgundy braid, 12"
   Gold paper cord leaves
   Tiny bell
Foam stamps:
   Acanthus Leaf
   Casablanca
Hot-glue gun & glue sticks
Paper wire
Papers:
   Corrugated, tan (1)
   Doily, square, ivory (1)
   Handmade, burgundy (1)
Pencil
Sandpaper, #600 fine-grit
Sponge brushes

INSTRUCTIONS

Prepare Surface:
1. Refer to Preparing Surfaces
on page 14. Prepare plate.

2. Using sponge brush, base-
coat front of plate with two
coats French Vanilla, sanding
between coats. Let dry.

Stamp:
1. Refer to Stamping on page
22. Using Acanthus Leaf stamp,
stamp around plate border
with Pure Gold Metallic. Let dry.

2. Using Casablanca stamp,
stamp handmade and corru-
gated papers with Inca Gold.

Prepare & Adhere Prints:
1. Refer to Preparing Prints for
Découpage on page 15. Tear
handmade paper into a circle
to cover center of plate. Using
decorative-edged scissors, cut
torn circle in half.

2. Cut two corners from doily.
Cut a curved strip of corrugated
paper.

3. Cut out photocopy and
memorabilia prints to fit in
center of plate.

4. Refer to Applying Prints on
pages 16–17. Layer handmade
paper, doily, corrugated, photocopy, and memorabilia on top
of one another. Using sponge
brush, adhere papers together
with découpage finish. Allow
different paper edges to peek
out around the plate.

5. Mix Inca Gold and water
(1:3). Using sponge brush,
cover entire paper area with
Inca Gold mixture to give an
aged look.

Finish:
1. Using sponge brush, cover
entire plate with two coats
découpage finish to seal.
Let dry.

2. Refer to Adding 3-D Accents
on page 20. Using hot-glue
gun, adhere burgundy braid
onto top left corner of plate,
securing ends onto back.

3. Twist wire around pencil
and pull out to desired length.

4. Refer to Adding 3-D Accents
on page 20. Adhere wire, bell,
berries, heart, and leaves onto
center of braid.

Memory Box

Pictured on page 65

Designed by
Susan Lowenthal

GATHER THESE SUPPLIES

Surface:
Papier-maché box, oval

Prints:
Anaglyphic wallpaper border
   (paintable)
Color photocopy of sepia-
   toned photograph

Other Supplies:
Acrylic craft paints:
   Antique Gold
   Baby Blue
   Patina
   Rose Chiffon
   Wicker White
Brushes:
   1" Flat
   #4 Fan
   Sponge(s)
Découpage finish
Matte acrylic sealer
Ruler
Sandpaper, #600 fine-grit
Sponge
Spray fixative

Continued on page 66

Memories of
Mother Plate
Instructions begin
on page 64

Memory
Box
Instructions begin
on page 64

THE OLD MELODEON

Continued from page 64

INSTRUCTIONS

Prepare Surface:
1. Refer to Preparing Surfaces on page 14. Prepare box.

2. Using 1" flat brush, basecoat box with two coats Wicker White, sanding between coats. Let dry.

Prepare & Adhere Prints:
1. Refer to Preparing Prints for Découpage on page 15. Cut strip of wallpaper border to fit around box sides.

2. Using ruler, cut straight piece of trim from wallpaper border to fit around box lid edge. Cut several raised motifs from wallpaper border and set aside.

3. Refer to Applying Prints on pages 16–17. Using sponge brush, adhere cutouts onto box with découpage finish. Let dry.

Paint:
1. Mix Baby Blue and water (1:3) and Rose Chiffon and water (1:3). Using fan brush, cover box in a daubing and sweeping motion, alternating with Baby Blue mixture and Rose Chiffon mixture.

Note: Do not cover entire box.

2. Using sponge, immediately wipe most paint off.

3. Sparingly highlight raised parts of paper with Antique Gold and Patina and immediately wipe off. Let dry.

4. Sparingly highlight raised motifs, set aside earlier, with Antique Gold and Patina and immediately wipe off. Let dry.

Finish:
1. Cut photograph into oval shape. Spray with workable fixative. Let dry.

2. Using sponge brush, adhere photograph and raised motif cutouts onto top of box lid with découpage finish.

3. Cover entire box lid with découpage finish. Let dry overnight.

4. Using sponge brush, cover entire box with matte acrylic sealer. Let dry.

Photograph Holder

Pictured on page 67

Designed by
Julie Watkins Schreiner

GATHER THESE SUPPLIES

Surface:
Silver guest towel stand

Prints:
Color photocopies of nature cards, 4" x 5¾" (Reverse any copies with text.) (2)

Other Supplies:
Craft glue
Fabrics:
  Aqua, 6½" x 9½" (2)
  White, 6½" x 9½" (2)
  (or colors that coordinate with photograph or print)
Fusible bonding web, ½"-wide
Gold grommets, ⅜" (6)
Grommet pliers kit
Iron
Loose-leaf rings, 1" (6)
Needle
Photograph transfer medium, clear
Silver metallic thread, #16
Sponge brush

INSTRUCTIONS

Prepare Surface:
1. Refer to Preparing Surfaces on page 14. Prepare stand.

2. Turn under edges of aqua fabric pieces ½". Using iron, hem fabric with fusible bonding web, following manufacturer's instructions.

3. Apply three grommets to top of each hemmed fabric piece, ½" from the end, following manufacturer's instructions.

Prepare & Adhere Prints:
1. Refer to Découpaging on Fabric on page 19. Using sponge brush, transfer photocopies onto centers of white fabric pieces with photograph transfer medium.

2. Refer to Preparing Prints for Découpage on page 15. Cut out transfers to exact photograph or card size.

Finish:
1. Adhere transfers onto centers of aqua fabric pieces with craft glue. Let dry.

2. Using needle, sew across four corners of transfers with metallic thread.

3. Place loose-leaf rings through grommet holes and slide onto sides of towel bar.

Photograph
Holder

Instructions begin
on page 66

Vintage Photograph Room Divider

*Designed by
Kathi Malarchuk Bailey*

GATHER THESE SUPPLIES

Surface:
Fabric room divider

Prints:
Color photocopies of
photographs (15)

Other Supplies:
Acrylic craft paints:
 Asphaltum
 Burnt Sienna
 Pure Gold
Brushes:
 Liner
 Sponge
Disposable bowls
Photograph transfer medium,
 clear
Sea sponge
Spray bottle
Stamping block:
 Ivy

INSTRUCTIONS

Prepare Surface:
1. Refer to Preparing Surfaces
on page 14. Prepare screen.

Prepare & Adhere Prints:
1. Refer to Preparing Prints for
Découpage on page 15. Plan
photograph placement on
fabric.

2. Refer to Découpaging on
Fabric on page 19. Using
sponge brush, transfer photocopies onto fabric with photograph transfer medium.
Let dry.

Paint:
1. Refer to Sponging Background on page 20. In two
separate disposable bowls,
mix Burnt Sienna and
Asphaltum with water (1:3).

2. Using spray bottle with
water, moisten fabric areas
where you will be placing paint.

3. Press damp sponge onto
moistened fabric with Burnt
Sienna mixture so color
spreads over fabric.

Note: Avoid hard edges or
strong color spots. If this
happens, spray with water.

4. Press damp sponge onto
moistened fabric with
Asphaltum mixture, so color
spreads over fabric.

Stamp:
1. Refer to Stamping on page
22. Using Ivy block, stamp
onto fabric with Pure Gold.

Finish:
1. Using liner, paint stems and
vines on ivy with Pure Gold.
Let dry.

Vintage Photograph
Room Divider

Wedding Plaque

Pictured on page 71

Designed by
Pat McIntosh

GATHER THESE SUPPLIES

Surface:
Wooden plaque

Print:
Wedding invitation photo-
copied onto parchment

Other Supplies:
Acrylic craft paints:
  Burnt Sienna
  Licorice
  Taffy
  Coordinating paint colors
Brushes:
  #4 Flat brush
  Sponge(s)
Cellulose sponge
Découpage finish
Sandpaper, #600 fine-grit

INSTRUCTIONS

Prepare Surface:
1. Refer to Preparing Surfaces
on page 14. Prepare plaque.

2. Using sponge brush, base-
coat plaque with two coats
Taffy, sanding between coats.
Let dry.

3. Trim edges with Licorice.

4. Refer to Sponging Background on page 20. Using
sponge, add texture over entire plaque with Burnt Sienna.

Prepare & Adhere Print:
1. Refer to Preparing Prints for
Découpage on page 15. Cut
out invitation to fit plaque.

2. Refer to Applying Prints on
pages 16–17. Using sponge
brush, adhere cutout onto
plaque with découpage finish.
Let dry.

Paint:
1. Refer to Tracing & Transferring Patterns on page 13.

Transfer Wedding Plaque
Pattern onto plaque.

2. Using flat brush, paint roses
and ribbon with colors match-
ing couple's wedding colors or
adhere print of choice. Let dry.

Finish:
1. Using sponge brush, cover
plaque with découpage finish
to seal. Let dry.

Wedding Plaque Pattern

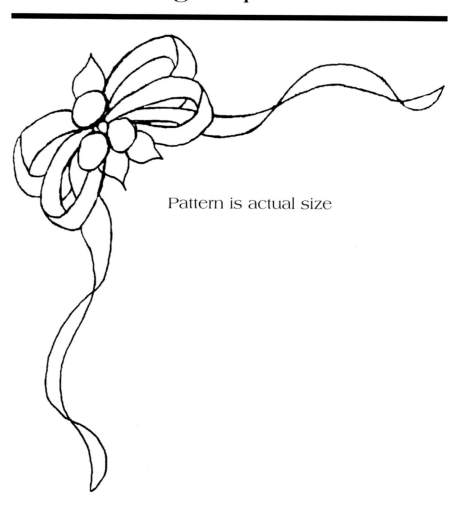

Pattern is actual size

Wedding Plaque
Instructions begin on page 70

Mrs. John David Grenga, senior

requests the pleasure of your company

at the wedding reception of her daughter

Josephine Trevette

and

Mr. Gary Wayne Lang

Saturday, the sixth of November

One thousand nine hundred and ninety-nine

at twelve o'clock

at the family's home

4830 Guerry Drive

Macon, Georgia

Picture Frame

Pictured on page 73

Designed by
Kathi Malarchuk Bailey

GATHER THESE SUPPLIES

Surface:
Unfinished wooden picture
frame, 8" x 10"

Prints:
Friendship-themed sayings
and flowers from cards

Other Supplies:
Acrylic craft paint:
Yellow Light
Découpage finish
Sandpaper, #600 fine-grit
Sponge brushes

INSTRUCTIONS

Prepare Surface:
1. Refer to Preparing Surfaces
on page 14. Prepare frame.

2. Using sponge brush, base-
coat entire frame with two
coats Yellow Light, sanding
between coats. Let dry.

Prepare & Adhere Prints:
1. Refer to Preparing Prints for
Découpage on page 15. Cut
out sayings and flower motifs.

2. Refer to Applying Prints on
pages 16–17. Using sponge
brush, adhere cutouts onto
frame with découpage finish.
Let dry.

Finish:
1. Using sponge brush, cover
entire frame with two coats
découpage finish to seal.
Let dry.

2. Using black marker, outline
flowers and add swirl centers.

Baby Book

Pictured on page 73

Designed by
Kathi Malarchuk Bailey

GATHER THESE SUPPLIES

Surface:
Unfinished wooden book

Prints:
Baby announcement
Baby-themed wrapping paper

Other Supplies:
Acrylic craft paints:
Light Periwinkle
Pure Gold
Wicker White
Brushes:
¼" Stencil
Sponge(s)
Découpage finish
Metallic gold permanent pen,
fine-point
Sandpaper, #600 fine-grit

INSTRUCTIONS

Prepare Surface:
1. Refer to Preparing Surfaces
on page 14. Prepare book.

2. Using sponge brush, base-
coat entire book with two
coats Wicker White, sanding
between coats. Let dry.

3. Base-coat book binding with
Light Periwinkle. Let dry.

Prepare & Adhere Prints:
1. Refer to Preparing Prints for
Découpage on page 15. Cut
out wrapping paper to fit front
and back covers of book.

2. Refer to Applying Prints on
pages 16–17. Adhere cutouts
onto book with découpage
finish. Let dry.

3. Cut out baby announcement
and adhere onto front cover
with découpage finish.

Finish:
1. Using gold pen, write baby's
name on book binding and
add horizontal lines and hearts
for decoration.

2. Refer to Stenciling on page
21. Using stencil brush, highlight outside page edges with
Pure Gold.

3. Cover entire book with two
coats découpage finish to seal.
Let dry.

Picture Frame
Instructions begin on page 72

Baby Book
Instructions begin on page 72

Découpage has resurfaced as a strong trend in home-fashion designs. Adaptable to almost any surface, découpage creates unlimited possibilities for designing a striking, one-of-a-kind piece, or establishing a decorative theme throughout an entire room.

Wine Bucket

Pictured on page 75

Designed by
Julie Watkins Schreiner

GATHER THESE SUPPLIES

Surface:
White metal bucket, 12½" tall

Print:
Photocopy of black-and-white
  plums print

Other Supplies:
Acrylic craft paints:
    Basil Green
    Licorice
Brushes:
    ½" Flat
    Sponge(s)
Colored pencils
Découpage finish
Gold paint marker, wide-tip
Masking tape, ¾"-wide
Matte acrylic sealer
Ruler

INSTRUCTIONS

Prepare Surface:
1. Refer to Preparing Surfaces on page 14. Prepare bucket.

2. Using masking tape, mask-off top and bottom rims of bucket.

3. Using sponge brush, base-coat bucket with Licorice. Let dry and remove tape.

4. Measure and mask-off rectangle 6" tall, 5" across at top, and 4" across at bottom in center of container.

5. Using flat brush, paint rectangle with Basil Green. Let dry and remove tape.

6. Spray entire container with matte acrylic sealer. Let dry.

Prepare & Adhere Print:
1. Using colored pencils, lightly shade parts of black-and-white motif.

2. Refer to Preparing Prints for Découpage on page 15. Cut out plum motif.

3. Refer to Applying Prints on pages 16–17. Using sponge brush, adhere cutout over green rectangle with découpage finish. Let dry.

4. Cover printed area with one coat découpage finish. Let dry.

Finish:
1. Using gold marker, draw decorative designs and lines on black borders of bucket.

2. Draw a borderline around base and around green rectangle.

3. Write plum name under découpaged motif.

4. Spray with matte acrylic sealer.

Wine Bucket
Instructions begin
on page 74

La Royale

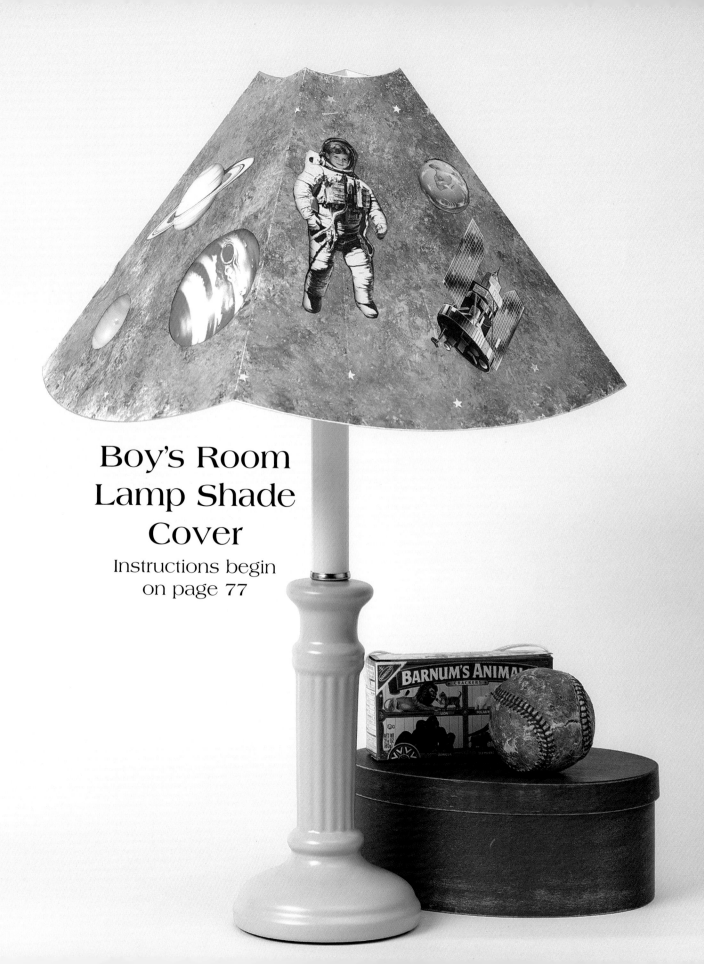

Boy's Room Lamp Shade Cover

Instructions begin
on page 77

Boy's Room Lamp Shade Cover

Pictured on page 76

Designed by
Susan Lowenthal

GATHER THESE SUPPLIES

Surface:
Pop-up paper lamp shade

Prints:
Color photocopies or prints of
astronauts, children, planets,
spaceships

Other Supplies:
Acrylic craft paints:
Blue Ribbon
French Blue
Silver Sterling
Wicker White
Brayer
Découpage finish
Old toothbrush
Paper punch: ¼" star
Sea sponge
Silver paint pen
Sponge brush
Spray fixative
Velcro®, self-adhesive

INSTRUCTIONS

Prepare Surface:
1. Refer to Preparing Surfaces
on page 14. Prepare shade.

2. Open and lay out shade on
flat, protected surface. Using
paper punch, punch stars
around shade top and bottom
in a zigzag pattern.

Note: Use fold lines as a guide
for even spacing.

Paint:
1. Refer to Sponging Background on page 20. Using
damp sponge, lightly sponge
background with Blue Ribbon,
French Blue, and Wicker
White to achieve an outer-space look.

2. Using old toothbrush, spatter shade with Silver Sterling
to resemble stars. Let dry.

Prepare & Adhere Prints:
1. Refer to Preparing Prints
for Découpage on page 15.
Cut out space motifs and
child's face.

2. Spray shade and cutout
backs with fixative. Let dry.

3. Refer to Applying Prints on
pages 16–17. Using brayer,
adhere cutouts onto shade.

Note: This will help the paper
to stretch and eliminate air
bubbles.

4. Place child's face in astronaut's headgear. Let dry.

Finish:
1. Using sponge brush, cover
entire shade with découpage
finish. Let dry.

2. Using silver pen, cover top
and bottom rims of shade.

3. Adhere Velcro onto back
edges of shade to keep it
closed.

Angel Bottle

Pictured on page 79

Designed by
Chris Adams, SCD

GATHER THESE SUPPLIES

Surface:
Glass bottle with cap, 9" tall

Print:
Angel print wrapping paper or
tissue paper

Other Supplies:
Acrylic craft paints:
Antique Gold
Pure Gold
Acrylic sealer spray
Brass bow charm
Foam stamp:
Medallion design
Découpage finish
Gold glitter
Gold rickrack, 30"
Hot-glue gun & glue sticks
Pencil
Silver paper wire, 12"
Sponge brushes

INSTRUCTIONS

Prepare Surface:
1. Refer to Preparing Surfaces
on page 14. Prepare bottle.

2. Refer to Stamping on page
22. Using medallion stamp,
randomly stamp bottle with
Antique Gold and Pure Gold.

3. Using sponge brush, paint
cap gold. Let dry.

Prepare & Adhere Prints:
1. Refer to Preparing Prints for
Découpage on page 15. Cut
out large angel, two medium
angels, and three small angels.
Continued on page 78

Continued from page 77

2. Refer to Applying Prints on pages 16–17. Using sponge brush, adhere large cutout onto center front of bottle with découpage finish. Let dry.

3. Adhere two medium angels onto bottle, placing them on either side of large angel at bottle base. Adhere three small angels onto back of bottle.

Finish:
1. Cover bottle and bottle cap with découpage finish. Sprinkle with glitter, removing excess from angel faces.

2. Spray entire bottle with acrylic spray sealer for a frosted look.

3. Tie rickrack around bottle neck and leave ends hanging.

4. Make two or three coils by twisting wire around pencil and pulling to desired length.

5. Refer to Adding 3-D Accents on page 20. Using hot-glue gun, adhere silver spirals and brass bow charm onto bottle neck where rickrack is tied.

Fruit Topiary

Pictured on page 79

Designed by
Marianne Ajamy

GATHER THESE SUPPLIES

Surfaces:
Plastic foam cone, 4" x 9"
Small wooden finial
Tin cachepot, 3" x 5"

Print:
Fruit print tissue paper

Other Supplies:
Acrylic craft paint:
    Antique Gold
Découpage finish
Green floral-foam block
Hot-glue gun & glue sticks
Sandpaper, #600 fine-grit
Spanish moss
Sponge brushes
Wooden dowel, ¼" dia., 6"

INSTRUCTIONS

Prepare Surfaces:
1. Refer to Preparing Surfaces on page 14. Prepare cone, finial, and cachepot.

2. Using sponge brush, base-coat cachepot and finial with two coats Antique Gold, sanding between coats. Let dry.

Prepare & Adhere Prints:
1. Refer to Preparing Prints for Découpage on page 15. Cut out fruit motifs from tissue.

2. Refer to Applying Prints on pages 16–17. Layer and adhere cutouts onto cone with découpage finish. Let dry.

3. Adhere fruit cutouts onto cachepot sides with découpage finish. Let dry.

Finish:
1. Push cone into cache-pot and insert dowel in center. Insert top of dowel into bottom of cone, leaving 1" of dowel exposed. Place Spanish moss around top of container to cover cone and dowel.

2. Using hot-glue gun, adhere finial onto top of cone.

Napkin Holder

Pictured on page 79

Designed by
Marianne Ajamy

GATHER THESE SUPPLIES

Surface:
Wooden napkin holder

Print:
Floral print wrapping paper or tissue paper

Other Supplies:
Acrylic craft paints:
    Antique Gold
    Autumn Leaves
    Dark Brown
    Mushroom
Découpage finish
Gold paint pen
Sandpaper, #600 fine-grit
Sea sponge
Sponge brushes

INSTRUCTIONS

Prepare Surface:
1. Refer to Preparing Surfaces on page 14. Prepare napkin holder.

2. Using sponge brush, base-coat outside and edges of napkin holder with two coats Antique Gold, sanding between coats. Let dry.

3. Refer to Sponging Background on page 20. Using damp sponge, alternately daub Autumn Leaves, Dark Brown, and Mushroom, creating tortoiseshell effect. Let dry.

Continued on page 80

Angel Bottle
Instructions begin
on page 77

Fruit Topiary
Instructions begin
on page 78

Napkin Holder
Instructions begin
on page 78

Fruit Box
Instructions
begin on
page 80

Continued from page 78

Prepare & Adhere Prints:
1. Refer to Preparing Prints for Découpage on page 15. Cut out flower motif.

2. Refer to Applying Prints on pages 16–17. Using sponge brush, adhere cutout onto front of napkin holder with découpage finish. Let dry.

Finish:
1. Using gold pen, outline flower motif.

Fruit Box

Pictured on page 79

Designed by
Chris Adams, SCD

GATHER THESE SUPPLIES

Surface:
Box, 6½" oval

Print:
Fruit print wrapping paper

Other Supplies:
Acrylic craft paints:
   Antique Copper
   Aquamarine
   Silver Sterling
Acrylic sealer spray
Copper wire, #20, 12"
Découpage finish
Hot-glue gun & glue sticks
Pencil
Sea sponge
Small artificial berry sprig
Sponge brushes
Texture paste

INSTRUCTIONS

Prepare Surface:
1. Refer to Preparing Surfaces on page 14. Prepare box.

2. Using sponge brush, cover box sides and lid with texture paste.

3. Using sponge, quickly press and lift over surface, leaving sandy texture.

4. Using sponge brush, cover top of lid with texture paste as if frosting a cake. Let dry.

5. Using sponge, lightly sponge over box with Antique Copper, Aquamarine, and Silver Sterling, one at a time, for a mottled effect. Let dry.

Prepare & Adhere Prints:
1. Refer to Preparing Prints for Découpage on page 15. Cut out fruit motifs.

2. Refer to Applying Prints on pages 16–17. Using sponge brush, adhere cutouts onto box and lid with découpage finish, allowing pieces to overlap edges of lid and box.

3. Using sponge, lightly sponge over cutouts with Antique Copper, Aquamarine, and Silver Sterling to slightly mute colors. Let dry.

4. Using sponge brush, cover two coats découpage finish. Let dry.

5. Spray with acrylic sealer.

Finish:
1. Make coils by twisting wire around pencil and pulling to get desired length.

2. Refer to Adding 3-D Accents on page 20. Using hot-glue gun, adhere coils and berry sprig onto box top.

Tissue Box

Pictured on page 81

Designed by
Marianne Ajamy

GATHER THESE SUPPLIES

Surface:
Clear plastic tissue box

Print:
Floral print fabric or paper

Other Supplies:
Découpage finish
Gold paint pen
Matte knife
Ruler
Sponge brushes

INSTRUCTIONS

Prepare Surface:
1. Refer to Preparing Surfaces on page 14. Prepare box.

Prepare & Adhere Prints:
1. Refer to Preparing Prints for Découpage on page 15. Measure and cut five squares from fabric or paper to fit box sides and top.

2. Refer to Applying Prints on pages 16–17. Using sponge brush, adhere cutouts onto box with découpage finish. Let dry.

Finish:
1. Using matte knife, cut tissue opening in box top.

2. Using gold pen, outline selected flowers on box.

Tissue Box

Instructions begin
on page 80

Desert Dreams Pillow
Instructions begin on page 83

Desert Dreams Pillow

Pictured on page 82

Designed by
Julie Watkins Schreiner

GATHER THESE SUPPLIES

Surface:
Lavender satin pillow

Print:
Color photocopy of greeting
   card, 7" x 4¾"

Other Supplies:
Acrylic craft paint:
   Pure Gold
Fabric glue
Fabrics:
   Orange, 6" x 8"
   Purple, 9½" x 10½"
   White, 8" x 5"
Fusible bonding web, ½"-wide
Iron
Photograph transfer medium,
   clear
Stencil:
   Primitive Icons
Stencil brush, ¼"

INSTRUCTIONS

Prepare Surface:
1. Refer to Preparing Surfaces
on page 14. Prepare pillow.

2. Refer to Preparing Prints for
Découpage on page 15. Trim
photocopy, leaving ¼" border
around motif.

Prepare & Adhere Prints:
1. Refer to Découpaging on
Fabric on page 19. Transfer
photocopy onto center of
white fabric with photograph
transfer medium, following
manufacturer's instructions.
Let dry.

2. Cut out motif to exact size
of original.

3. Turn under edges of orange
and purple fabrics ½".

4. Using iron, hem edges with
fusible bonding web, following
manufacturer's instructions.

Stencil:
1. Refer to Stenciling on page
21. Using stencil brush, randomly stencil Primitive Icons
on purple fabric with Pure
Gold. Let dry.

Finish:
1. Adhere purple fabric onto
pillow with fabric glue.

2. Adhere motif onto center of
orange fabric.

3. Adhere orange fabric onto
purple patch.

Floral Frame

Pictured on pages 84–85

Designed by
Susan Dumas

GATHER THESE SUPPLIES

Surface:
Wooden picture frame

Prints:
Floral print wallpaper
Striped wallpaper

Other Supplies:
Acrylic craft paint:
   Wicker White
Cloth
Découpage finish
Drawer pull
Drill & ¼" drill bit
Hot-glue gun & glue sticks
Sea sponge
Sponge brushes
Trim
Wallpaper paste
Wallpaper smoothing tool
Wooden dowel, ¼" (6")

INSTRUCTIONS

Prepare Surface:
1. Refer to Preparing Surfaces
on page 14. Prepare frame.

Prepare & Adhere Prints:
1. Refer to Preparing Prints for
Découpage on page 15. Cut
one piece from each wallpaper
to cover half of frame, allowing
extra to cover frame edges.

2. Adhere cutouts onto frame
with wallpaper paste.

Continued on page 86

Floral Frame

Instructions begin on page 83

Tassel Box

Instructions begin on page 86

Continued from page 83

3. Using wallpaper smoothing tool and cloth, smooth paper surface and remove excess paste.

4. Using damp sponge, wipe wallpaper to remove excess paste.

5. Refer to Applying Prints on pages 16–17. Using sponge brush, cover papered surfaces with découpage finish. Let dry.

Finish:
1. Using sponge brush, cover drawer pull with Wicker White. Let dry.

2. Drill ¼" holes at bottom of frame to insert drawer pull. Using hot-glue gun, adhere pull.

3. Refer to Adding 3-D Accents on page 20. Using hot-glue gun, adhere trim around inside of frame.

4. Drill ½"-deep hole in center back bottom of frame and insert dowel to support frame and keep it upright.

Tassel Box

Pictured on pages 84–85

Designed by
Susan Dumas

GATHER THESE SUPPLIES

Surface:
Wooden box, 8½" square

Prints:
Floral print wallpaper
Striped wallpaper

Other Supplies:
Acrylic craft paints:
    Leaf Green
    Wicker White
Buttons (2)
Carpenter's glue
Cloth
Découpage finish
Drawer pull
Drill & ¼" drill bit
Hot-glue gun & glue sticks
Sea sponge
Sponge brushes
Tassel trim and braid
Wallpaper paste
Wallpaper smoothing tool
Wooden drawer knobs,
    round (4)

INSTRUCTIONS

Prepare Surface:
1. Refer to Preparing Surfaces on page 14. Prepare box.

Prepare & Adhere Prints:
1. Cut two 8½"-square pieces of floral wallpaper. Cut two 8½"-square pieces of striped wallpaper.

2. Adhere floral pieces onto two opposite sides of box with wallpaper paste. Adhere striped wallpaper onto other two sides.

3. Using wallpaper smoothing tool and cloth, smooth paper surface and remove excess paste.

4. Using damp sponge, wipe wallpaper to remove excess.

5. Cut out four triangular-shaped pieces of floral wallpaper and adhere onto striped wallpaper so points meet in center.

6. Adhere floral wallpaper onto lid top and sides, using one long strip for the edges.

7. Refer to Applying Prints on pages 16–17. Using sponge brush, cover papered surfaces with découpage finish. Let dry.

Finish:
1. Using sponge brush, cover knobs with Leaf Green. Let dry.

2. Adhere knobs onto bottom corners of box with carpenter's glue for feet.

3. Using sponge brush, cover drawer pull with Wicker White.

4. Drill ¼" holes in box lid to insert drawer pull.

5. Refer to Adding 3-D Accents on page 20. Using hot-glue gun, adhere tassel trim and braid around sides of lid and bottom of box.

6. Adhere buttons onto sides of box where paper triangles meet in center.

Glass Birthday Plate

Instructions begin on page 88

Glass Birthday Plate

Pictured on page 87

Designed by
Kathi Malarchuk Bailey

GATHER THESE SUPPLIES

Surface:
Glass plate, 10" dia.

Print:
Birthday card

Other Supplies:
Acrylic craft paint:
  Licorice
Cellulose sponge, 1" square
Découpage finish
Gold foil kit
Paper towels
Rubbing alcohol
Sponge brushes

INSTRUCTIONS

Prepare Surface:
1. Refer to Preparing Surfaces on page 14. Prepare plate.

2. Using paper towels, clean plate with rubbing alcohol. Let dry.

Prepare & Adhere Print:
1. Refer to Preparing Prints for Découpage on page 15. Cut out birthday card motif.

2. Refer to Reverse Découpaging on page 19. Turn plate upside down. Using sponge brush, adhere motif onto plate back with découpage finish.

Apply Gold Foil:
1. Refer to Tracing and Transferring Patterns on page 13. Transfer birthday saying onto paper.

2. Turn plate over and using tip of foil kit adhesive bottle, outline saying. Let dry until clear.

3. Using damp sponge, sponge plate back with foil adhesive. Let dry until clear.

4. Apply gold foil over sponged areas and lettering, following manufacturer's instructions.

Finish:
1. Using sponge brush, cover plate back with Licorice. Let dry two hours.

2. Refer to Applying Prints on pages 16–17. Using sponge brush, cover plate back with two coats découpage finish to seal. Let dry.

Funky Flower Table

Pictured on page 89

Designed by
Sandra McCooey

GATHER THESE SUPPLIES

Surface:
Unfinished wooden table

Prints:
Wrapping paper with flowers, hearts, leaves, and squiggles
Solid purple wrapping paper or craft paper

Other Supplies:
Acrylic craft paints:
  Green Clover
  Neon Yellow
Découpage finish
High-gloss acrylic sealer
Ruler
Sandpaper, #600 fine-grit
Sponge brushes

INSTRUCTIONS

Prepare Surface:
1. Refer to Preparing Surfaces on page 14. Prepare table.

2. Using sponge brush, base-coat tabletop and shelf with several coats Green Clover, sanding between coats. Let dry.

3. Base-coat table legs with several coats Neon Yellow, sanding between coats. Let dry.

Prepare & Adhere Prints:
1. Refer to Preparing Prints for Découpage on page 15. Cut out flower, heart, leaf, and squiggle motifs.

2. Tear 2½" strips of purple paper for tabletop and tear 1½" squares of purple paper for bottom shelf.

3. Refer to Applying Prints on pages 16–17. Using sponge brush, adhere purple strips onto tabletop and purple squares onto bottom shelf with découpage finish. Let dry.

4. Adhere other cutouts onto tabletop with découpage finish. Let dry.

Finish:
1. Using sponge brush, cover découpaged surfaces with two coats acrylic sealer to seal. Let dry.

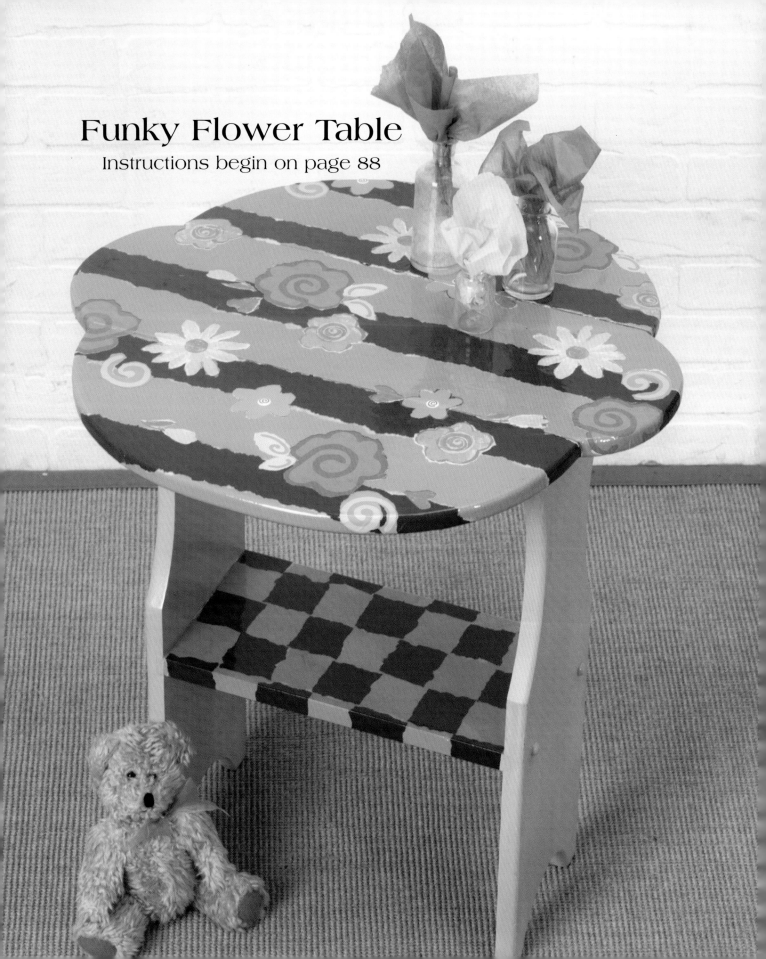

Funky Flower Table

Instructions begin on page 88

Pressed Flowers
Lamp Shade

Instructions begin
on page 91

Pressed Flowers Lamp Shade

Pictured on page 90

Designed by
Pat McIntosh

GATHER THESE SUPPLIES

Surface:
Light-colored lamp shade

Prints:
Assorted pressed flowers

Other Supplies:
Découpage finish
Sponge brush

INSTRUCTIONS

Prepare Surface:
1. Refer to Preparing Surfaces on page 14. Prepare shade.

Prepare & Adhere Prints:
1. Refer to Applying Prints on pages 16–17. Using sponge brush, adhere flowers onto outside of shade with découpage finish. Let dry.

Finish:
1. Cover entire shade with découpage finish to seal. Let dry.

Serving Tray

Pictured on pages 92–93

Designed by
Lauren Powell

GATHER THESE SUPPLIES

Surface:
Wooden frame with glass

Print:
Fabric of choice (size of frame)

Other Supplies:
Acrylic craft paint:
   Antique Gold
Black spray paint
Découpage finish
Drawer pulls (2)
Fabric trim
Hot-glue gun & glue sticks
Plywood, ¼"-thick, cut to fit
   frame size
Sandpaper, #600 fine-grit
Screwdriver
Small nails
Small saw
Small screws (2)
Sponge brushes
Tack hammer

INSTRUCTIONS

Prepare Surface:
1. Refer to Preparing Surfaces on page 14. Prepare frame.

2. Using sponge brush, base-coat frame with two coats Antique Gold, sanding between coats. Let dry.

3. Refer to Adding 3-D Accents on page 20. Using hot-glue gun, adhere trim onto top of frame.

Prepare & Adhere Print:
1. Refer to Preparing Prints for Découpage on page 15. Prepare and cut fabric.

2. Refer to Découpaging on Fabric on page 19. Adhere fabric onto plywood with découpage finish. Let dry.

3. Trim excess fabric from edges. Insert glass into frame and lay fabric-covered board behind glass.

Finish:
1. Cut four triangular plywood pieces for corners on back.

2. Using tack hammer, secure triangles to frame with small nails.

3. Spray door handles with Black. Let dry.

4. Center and gently screw handles on frame side so as not to fracture glass.

Serving Tray

Instructions begin on page 91

Dried Leaves
Lamp Shade

Instructions begin
on page 95

Dried Leaves Lamp Shade

Pictured on page 94

Designed by
Pat McIntosh

GATHER THESE SUPPLIES

Surface:
Light-colored lamp shade

Prints:
Assorted pressed leaves

Other Supplies:
Découpage finish
Sponge brush

INSTRUCTIONS

Prepare Surface:
1. Refer to Preparing Surfaces on page 14. Prepare shade.

Prepare & Adhere Prints:
1. Refer to Applying Prints on pages 16–17. Using sponge brush, adhere leaves onto inside of shade with découpage finish. Let dry.

Finish:
1. Cover inside of shade with one coat découpage finish to seal. Let dry.

Galvanized Planter

Pictured on pages 96–97

Designed by
Ann Barnes

GATHER THESE SUPPLIES

Surface:
Galvanized bucket, oblong

Prints:
Floral print greeting cards, note cards, or postcards

Other Supplies:
Acrylic craft paints:
   Basil Green
   Burnt Umber
   Linen
Découpage finish
Glazing medium
Masking tape
Raffia
Sponge brushes

INSTRUCTIONS

Prepare Surface:
1. Refer to Preparing Surfaces on page 14. Prepare bucket.

2. Using sponge brush, base-coat outside of bucket with two coats Linen. Let dry.

3. Using masking tape, mask-off areas to be striped and paint with Basil Green. Let dry and remove tape.

Prepare & Adhere Prints:
1. Refer to Preparing Prints for Découpage on page 15. Cut out card motifs.

2. Refer to Applying Prints on pages 16–17. Using sponge brush, adhere cutouts onto bucket with découpage finish. Let dry.

Antique:
1. Refer to Antiquing on page 18. Mix Burnt Umber and glazing medium (1:3). Using sponge brush, antique cutouts with Burnt Umber glazing mixture. Let dry.

Finish:
1. Cover planter with two coats découpage finish to seal. Let dry.

2. Accent bucket handles with raffia bows.

95

Galvanized Planter

Instructions begin on page 95

Botanical Insect Table

Pictured on page 99

Designed by
Lauren Powell

GATHER THESE SUPPLIES

Surface:
Wooden folding table

Prints:
Color photocopies of botanical
  insect postcards

Other Supplies:
Acrylic craft paint:
  Russet Brown
Brushes:
  3" Flat
  Sponge(s)
Découpage finish
Glazing medium
Latex paint:
  Basil Green
Matte acrylic sealer
Sandpaper, #600 fine-grit
Towel or sponge

INSTRUCTIONS

Prepare Surface:
1. Refer to Preparing Surfaces
on page 14. Prepare table.

2. Using sponge brush, base-
coat entire table with several
coats Basil Green, sanding
between coats. Let dry.

Prepare & Adhere Prints:
1. Refer to Preparing Prints for
Découpage on page 15. Cut
out postcards. Cut out a few
individual insects. Select
desired placement on table.

2. Refer to Applying Prints on
pages 16–17. Using sponge
brush, adhere postcards onto
tabletop with découpage
finish. Let dry.

3. Adhere insects among
postcards. Let dry.

4. Cover tabletop with découpage finish. Let dry.

Antique:
1. Refer to Antiquing on page
18. Mix Russet Brown with
glazing medium (1:2).

2. Using flat brush, cover table
with Russet Brown mixture. If
mixture is too dark over insect
postcards, use a damp towel
or sponge to wipe off excess.

3. Randomly sand table
edges, creating an aged
appearance.

Finish:
1. Spray table with several
coats matte acrylic sealer.

Butterfly Chair

Pictured on page 99

Designed by
Lauren Powell

GATHER THESE SUPPLIES

Surface:
Wooden folding chair

Prints:
Colored butterfly print
  wrapping paper

Other Supplies:
Acrylic craft paints:
  Fresh Foliage
  Lipstick Red
  Medium Yellow
  Periwinkle
Brushes:
  3" Flat
  Sponge(s)
Découpage finish
Latex paint:
  Black
Matte acrylic sealer
Sandpaper, #600 fine-grit

INSTRUCTIONS

Prepare Surface:
1. Refer to Preparing Surfaces
on page 14. Prepare chair.

2. Using sponge brush, base-
coat chair with Black. Let dry.

3. Randomly sand chair,
creating an aged appearance.

Prepare & Adhere Prints:
1. Refer to Applying Prints
on pages 16–17. Cut out
butterfly motifs.

2. Using sponge brush, adhere
cutouts onto chair with découpage finish.

3. Cover entire chair with one
coat découpage finish.
Let dry.

Paint:
1. Using handle end of flat
brush, randomly dot chair with
Fresh Foliage, Lipstick Red,
Medium Yellow, and Peri-
winkle. Let dry.

Finish:
1. Using sponge brush, cover
chair with several coats matte
acrylic sealer. Let dry.

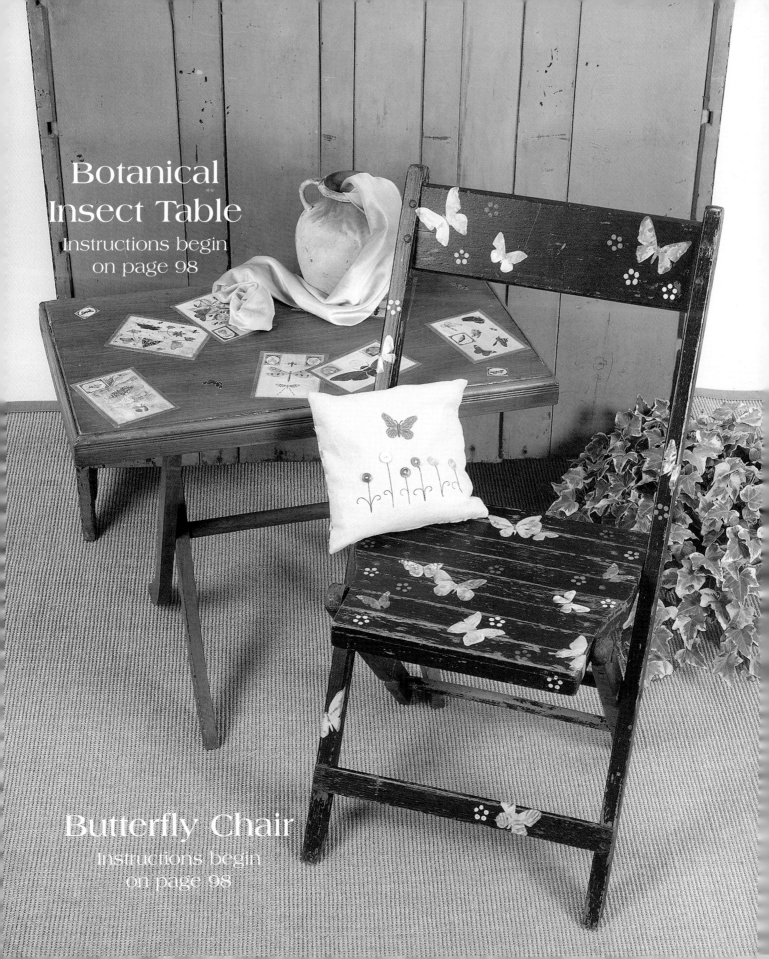

Botanical
Insect Table
Instructions begin
on page 98

Butterfly Chair
Instructions begin
on page 98

Friends Photograph Frame

Pictured on page 101

Designed by
Ann Barnes

GATHER THESE SUPPLIES

Surface:
Cardboard photograph frame
  5" x 7"

Prints:
Small floral prints

Other Supplies:
Acrylic craft paint:
  Mint Green
Antiquing medium:
  Down Home Brown
Découpage finish
Glazing medium
Metallic gold permanent pen
Sponge brushes
Thin gold braid
White craft glue

INSTRUCTIONS

Prepare Surface:
1. Refer to Preparing Surfaces on page 14. Prepare frame.

2. Using sponge brush, base-coat frame with Mint Green. Let dry.

Prepare & Adhere Prints:
1. Refer to Preparing Prints for Découpage on page 15. Cut out small floral motifs.

2. Refer to Applying Prints on pages 16–17. Using sponge brush, adhere cutouts onto frame corners with découpage finish. Let dry.

3. Cover entire frame with découpage finish to seal. Let dry.

4. Using gold pen, write "friends" at bottom of frame.

Antique:
1. Refer to Antiquing on page 18. Mix Down Home Brown with glazing medium (1:3). Using sponge brush, antique entire frame with Down Home Brown mixture. Let dry.

Finish:
1. Adhere gold braid onto top corners of frame with craft glue, using photograph on page 101 as a guide. Let dry.

Memories Photograph Album

Pictured on page 101

Designed by
Ann Barnes

GATHER THESE SUPPLIES

Surface:
Photograph album, single-photo size, mint green

Prints:
Small floral prints

Other Supplies:
Acrylic craft paint:
  Mint Green
Antiquing medium:
  Down Home Brown
Decorative satin trim
Découpage finish
Glazing medium
Metallic gold permanent pen
Sponge brushes
White craft glue

INSTRUCTIONS

Prepare Surface:
1. Refer to Preparing Surfaces on page 14. Prepare album.

2. Using sponge brush, base-coat album with Mint Green. Let dry.

Prepare & Adhere Prints:
1. Refer to Preparing Prints for Découpage on page 15. Cut out small floral motifs.

2. Refer to Applying Prints on pages 16–17. Using sponge brush, adhere cutouts onto album front with découpage finish. Let dry.

3. Cover entire album front with découpage finish to seal. Let dry.

4. Using gold pen, write "Memories Treasures" on album front.

Antique:
1. Refer to Antiquing on page 18. Mix Down Home Brown with glazing medium (1:3). Using sponge brush, antique entire album with Down Home Brown mixture. Let dry.

Finish:
1. Adhere trim onto album securing ends inside cover with craft glue, using photograph on page 101 as a guide. Let dry.

Friends Photograph Frame
Instructions begin on page 100

Memories Photograph Album
Instructions begin on page 100

Hydrangea
Casserole Carrier
Instructions begin on page 104

Hydrangea Casserole Carrier

Pictured on pages 102–103

Designed by
Marianne Ajamy

GATHER THESE SUPPLIES

Surface:
Lidded casserole carrier,
   rectangular

Print:
Floral print wrapping paper

Other Supplies:
Acrylic craft paint:
   Medium Gray
Découpage finish
Pearl-finish acrylic spray
Pearlizing medium
Sponge brushes

INSTRUCTIONS

Prepare Surface:
1. Refer to Preparing Surfaces on page 14. Prepare carrier.

2. Using sponge brush, base-coat entire carrier with Medium Gray. Let dry.

Prepare & Adhere Prints:
1. Refer to Preparing Prints for Découpage on page 15. Cut out floral motifs (enough to cover entire lid without overlapping).

2. Refer to Applying Prints on pages 16–17. Using sponge brush, adhere cutouts onto lid top with découpage finish. Let dry.

Finish:
1. Spray lid with pearl-finish acrylic.

2. Using sponge brush, cover carrier sides and handles with pearlizing medium.

Hibiscus Brooch

Pictured on page 105

Designed by
Pat McIntosh

GATHER THESE SUPPLIES

Surface:
Brooch base & pin back

Print:
Miniature hibiscus print

Other Supplies:
Acrylic craft paint:
   Licorice
Craft glue
Découpage finish
Matte acrylic sealer
Metallic gold wax finish
Soft cloth
Sponge brushes
Watercolor paper

INSTRUCTIONS

Prepare Surface:
1. Refer to Preparing Surfaces on page 14. Prepare brooch.

Prepare & Adhere Print:
1. Refer to Preparing Prints for Découpage on page 15. Cut out motif.

2. Spray entire brooch with matte acrylic sealer. Let dry.

3. Refer to Applying Prints on pages 16–17. Using sponge brush, adhere cutout onto brooch base with découpage finish. Let dry.

4. Cover brooch with several coats découpage finish. Let dry.

Finish:
1. Using soft cloth, rub edges of brooch with metallic gold wax, following manufacturer's instructions.

2. Cut out watercolor paper to fit back of brooch.

3. Using sponge brush, paint paper with Licorice. Let dry.

4. Adhere paper onto back of brooch with craft glue. Adhere pin back in place.

Floral Earrings
Instructions begin
on page 106

Floral Brooch
Instructions begin
on page 106

Hibiscus
Brooch
Instructions begin
on page 104

Angel Brooch
Instructions begin on page 106

Floral Earrings

Pictured on page 105

Designed by
Pat McIntosh

GATHER THESE SUPPLIES

Surface:
Earring bases & backs (2 each)

Prints:
Decorative paper napkins

Other Supplies:
Craft glue
Découpage finish
Sponge brush
Watercolor paper

INSTRUCTIONS

Prepare Surface:
1. Refer to Preparing Surfaces on page 14. Prepare earrings.

Prepare & Adhere Prints:
1. Refer to Preparing Prints for Découpage on page 15. Cut out motifs from paper napkin. Separate and discard inner layers.

2. Refer to Applying Prints on pages 16–17. Using sponge brush, adhere cutouts onto bases of earrings with découpage finish. Allow cutouts to wrap around to backs of earrings. Let dry.

3. Cover earrings with several coats découpage finish. Let dry.

Finish:
1. Cut out watercolor paper to fit earring backs.

2. Adhere paper onto earring backs with craft glue.

Floral Brooch

Pictured on page 105

Designed by
Pat McIntosh

GATHER THESE SUPPLIES

Surface:
Brooch base & pin back

Print:
Miniature floral print

Other Supplies:
Craft glue
Découpage finish
Matte acrylic sealer
Sponge brush

INSTRUCTIONS

Prepare Surface:
1. Refer to Preparing Surfaces on page 14. Prepare brooch.

Prepare & Adhere Print:
1. Refer to Preparing Prints for Découpage on page 15. Cut out selected motif and spray with matte acrylic sealer. Let dry.

2. Refer to Applying Prints on pages 16–17. Using sponge brush, adhere cutout onto brooch base with découpage finish.

Note: You may need to clip edges of print to get paper to bend to back side of brooch base.

3. Cover brooch with several coats découpage finish. Let dry.

Finish:
1. Adhere brooch back onto base with craft glue. Adhere pin back in place.

Angel Brooch

Pictured on page 105

Designed by
Pat McIntosh

GATHER THESE SUPPLIES

Surface:
Brooch base & pin back

Print:
Angel print tissue paper

Other Supplies:
Craft glue
Découpage finish
Matte acrylic sealer
Sponge brush

INSTRUCTIONS

Prepare Surface:
1. Refer to Preparing Surfaces on page 14. Prepare brooch.

Prepare & Adhere Print:
1. Refer to Preparing Prints for Découpage on page 15. Cut out selected motif and spray with matte acrylic sealer. Let dry.

2. Refer to Applying Prints on pages 16–17. Adhere cutout onto brooch base with découpage finish. Let dry.

3. Cover brooch with several coats découpage finish. Let dry.

Note: Do not worry if the tissue wrinkles a bit, as this will make it look antiqued.

Finish:
1. Adhere pin back onto brooch with craft glue.

Napkins make an ideal paper for découpage on cylinders such as candles and clay flowerpots due to their thinness and ability to wrap around curves easily. Today's napkin designs provide an endless number of motifs to choose from. The All-in-One finish works best for napkin crafting.

Fish Candle

Pictured on pages 108–109

Designed by
Pat McIntosh

GATHER THESE SUPPLIES

Surface:
Large blue-green pillar candle

Prints:
Fish print paper napkins

Other Supplies:
Acrylic craft paints:
  Brilliant Ultramarine
  Emerald Isle
  Sunflower
  Wicker White
Brushes:
  #4 Flat
  Sponge
Découpage finish

INSTRUCTIONS

Prepare Surface:
1. Refer to Preparing Surfaces on page 14. Prepare candle.

Prepare & Adhere Prints:
1. Refer to Preparing Prints for Découpage on page 15. Cut out fish motifs.

2. Refer to Découpaging on Candles on page 20. Using sponge brush, adhere cutouts onto candle with découpage finish.

Paint:
1. Double-load flat brush with Emerald Isle and Sunflower. Paint seaweed, using photograph on pages 108–109 as a guide.

2. Double-load flat brush with Brilliant Ultramarine and Wicker White. Paint more seaweed. Let dry.

Finish:
1. Using sponge brush, cover candle with two coats découpage finish. Let dry.

Fish Cabinet

Pictured on pages 108–109

Designed by
Pat McIntosh

GATHER THESE SUPPLIES

Surface:
Wooden cabinet

Print:
Tropical fish print wrapping
  paper

Other Supplies:
Acrylic craft paints:
  Coastal Blue
  Fresh Foliage
  Licorice
  Wicker White
Brushes:
  Round
  Sponge
Découpage finish
Sandpaper, #600 fine-grit

INSTRUCTIONS

Prepare Surface:
1. Refer to Preparing Surfaces on page 14. Prepare cabinet.

2. Using sponge brush, base-coat entire cabinet with two coats Coastal Blue, sanding between coats. Let dry.

Paint:
1. Paint trim with Licorice. Let dry.

2. Using round brush, paint seaweed on cabinet doors and sides with Fresh Foliage. Highlight with Wicker White.

Prepare & Adhere Prints:
1. Refer to Preparing Prints for Découpage on page 15. Cut out fish motifs.

2. Refer to Applying Prints on pages 16–17. Using sponge brush, adhere cutouts onto cabinet front, sides, and top with découpage finish.

Finish:
1. Using handle end of round brush, dot bubbles from fishes' mouths and to side trim with Wicker White.

2. Using round brush, paint wavy swirls at top and bottom with Wicker White. Let dry.

3. Using sponge brush, cover cabinet with two coats découpage finish to seal. Let dry.

Fish Candle
Instructions begin on page 107

Fish
Cabinet
Instructions begin
on page 107

Twisted-wire Candle

Pictured on page 111

Designed by
Kathi Malarchuk Bailey

GATHER THESE SUPPLIES

Surface:
Green pillar candle, round

Print:
Bright floral print paper napkin

Other Supplies:
Découpage finish
Silver wire, fine-gauge
Sponge brushes

INSTRUCTIONS

Prepare Surface:
1. Refer to Preparing Surfaces on page 14. Prepare candle.

Prepare & Adhere Print:
1. Refer to Preparing Prints for Découpage on page 15. Cut napkin to same height as candle. Separate and discard inner layers.

2. Refer to Découpaging on Candles on page 20. Using sponge brush, adhere napkin onto candle with découpage finish, trimming excess napkin where edges meet in back. Let dry 20 minutes.

3. Cover candle with two coats découpage finish. Let dry.

Finish:
1. Twist wire, winding it around candle sides.

Gingham Candle

Pictured on page 111

Designed by
Kathi Malarchuk Bailey

GATHER THESE SUPPLIES

Surface:
Large white pillar candle, square

Prints:
Gingham print paper napkins

Other Supplies:
Coordinating colored buttons (2)
Craft glue
Découpage finish
Sponge brushes

INSTRUCTIONS

Prepare Surface:
1. Refer to Preparing Surfaces on page 14. Prepare candle.

Prepare & Adhere Prints:
1. Refer to Preparing Prints for Découpage on page 15. Fold napkins into four triangles and cut triangles to fit around candle sides, allowing for overlapping. Separate and discard inner layers.

2. Refer to Applying Prints on pages 16–17. Using sponge brush, adhere napkins onto candle with découpage finish. Let dry 20 minutes.

3. Cover candle with two coats découpage finish. Let dry.

Finish:
1. Adhere buttons onto sides where napkin points meet with craft glue.

Twisted-wire Candle

Instructions begin on page 110

Gingham Candle

Instructions begin on page 110

White Roses Candle

Pictured on page 113

Designed by
Kathi Malarchuk Bailey

GATHER THESE SUPPLIES

Surface:
Large pillar candle, cream

Prints:
Metallic and floral print paper
  napkins

Other Supplies:
Brushes:
  Round
  Sponge
Découpage finish
Gold foil kit

INSTRUCTIONS

Prepare Surface:
1. Refer to Preparing Surfaces
on page 14. Prepare candle.

Prepare & Adhere Prints:
1. Refer to Preparing Prints for
Découpage on page 15. Cut
out rose motifs, leaving about
½" around edges. Separate and
discard inner layers.

2. Refer to Découpaging on
Candles on page 20. Using
sponge brush, cover entire
candle with découpage finish.
Press cutouts onto surface.
Let dry.

Finish:
1. Using handle end of round
brush, randomly dot on candle
with foil adhesive. Let dry until
clear.

2. Apply gold foil over
adhesive, following
manufacturer's instructions.

3. Cover candle with two
coats découpage finish to
seal. Let dry.

Dried Flowers Candle

Pictured on page 113

Designed by
Pat McIntosh

GATHER THESE SUPPLIES

Surface:
Pillar candle

Prints:
Variety of dried flowers

Other Supplies:
Découpage finish
Sponge brush

INSTRUCTIONS

Prepare Surface:
1. Refer to Preparing Surfaces
on page 14. Prepare candle.

Prepare & Adhere Prints:
1. Refer to Découpaging on
Candles on page 20. Using
sponge brush, cover entire
candle with découpage finish.
Press dried flowers to surface.
Let dry.

Finish:
1. Cover candle with two
coats découpage finish to
seal. Let dry.

Pink Roses Candle

Pictured on page 113

Designed by
Pat McIntosh

GATHER THESE SUPPLIES

Surface:
Pillar candle

Prints:
Pink rose print paper napkins

Other Supplies:
Découpage finish
Sponge brush

INSTRUCTIONS

Prepare Surface:
1. Refer to Preparing Surfaces
on page 14. Prepare candle.

Prepare & Adhere Prints:
1. Refer to Preparing Prints for
Découpage on page 15. Cut
out rose motifs. Separate and
discard inner layers.

2. Refer to Découpaging on
Candles on page 20. Using
sponge brush, cover entire
candle with découpage finish.
Press cutouts onto surface.
Let dry.

Finish:
1. Cover candle with two
coats découpage finish to
seal. Let dry.

White Roses Candle

Instructions begin on page 112

Dried Flowers
Candle

Instructions begin on page 112

Pink Roses
Candle

Instructions begin
on page 112

Birthday Balloons Pot

*Designed by
Pat McIntosh*

GATHER THESE SUPPLIES

Surface:
Clay pot

Prints:
Balloon print paper napkins

Other Supplies:
Acrylic craft paints:
  Licorice
  Wicker White
Black permanent marker
Brushes:
  ¼" Stencil
  Sponge
Découpage finish
Matte acrylic sealer
Sandpaper, #600 fine-grit
Stencil:
  Alphabet

INSTRUCTIONS

Prepare Surface:
1. Refer to Preparing Surfaces on page 14. Prepare pot.

2. Using sponge brush, base-coat pot with several coats Wicker White. Let dry.

Prepare & Adhere Prints:
1. Refer to Preparing Prints for Découpage on page 15. Cut out balloon motifs. Separate and discard inner layers.

2. Refer to Applying Prints on pages 16–17. Using sponge brush, adhere cutouts onto pot with découpage finish.

Note: Work in a small area at a time. If wrinkles occur, apply mild pressure with brush to remove wrinkle working from middle out to edges.

3. Cover pot with at least five coats découpage finish.
Let dry.

4. Lightly sand pot.

5. Using sponge brush, cover with one coat découpage finish.

Stencil:
1. Refer to Stenciling on page 21. Using alphabet stencil, stencil 'Birthday' around pot with Licorice.

2. Using marker, draw balloon strings.

Finish:
1. Spray outside pot with several coats matte acrylic sealer. Let dry between coats.

Note: If using clay pots for plants, it is recommended to use a plastic liner between the plant and inside of pot.

Birthday Balloons Pot

Fruit Pot
Instructions begin
on page 117

Fruit Pot

Pictured on page 116

Designed by
Pat McIntosh

GATHER THESE SUPPLIES

Surface:
Clay pot

Prints:
Fruit print paper napkins

Other Supplies:
Acrylic craft paints:
    Asphaltum
    Sunflower
    Wicker White
Cellulose sponge
Découpage finish
Matte acrylic sealer
Sandpaper, #600 fine-grit
Sponge brushes

INSTRUCTIONS

Prepare Surface:
1. Refer to Preparing Surfaces on page 14. Prepare pot.

2. Mix Wicker White and Sunflower (1:3) Using sponge brush, base-coat pot with several coats Wicker White/ Sunflower mixture, sanding between coats. Let dry.

Prepare & Adhere Prints:
1. Refer to Preparing Prints for Découpage on page 15. Cut out fruit motifs. Separate and discard inner layers.

2. Refer to Applying Prints on pages 16–17. Using sponge brush, adhere cutouts onto pot with découpage finish.

Note: Work in a small area at a time. If wrinkles occur, apply mild pressure with brush to remove wrinkle working from the middle out to the edges.

3. Cover pot with at least five coats découpage finish.
Let dry.

4. Lightly sand pot.

5. Using sponge brush, cover with one coat découpage finish.

Antique:
1. Refer to Antiquing on page 18. Mix Asphaltum with water (1:4). Using sponge, antique pot with Asphaltum mixture. Let dry.

Finish:
1. Spray outside of pot with several coats matte acrylic sealer. Let dry between coats.

Note: If using clay pots for plants, it is recommended to use a plastic liner between the plant and inside of pot.

Chicken Pot

Pictured on page 118

Designed by
Pat McIntosh

GATHER THESE SUPPLIES

Surface:
Clay pot

Prints:
Chicken print paper napkins

Other Supplies:
Acrylic craft paints:
    Raw Sienna
    Sunflower
    Taffy
Découpage finish
Sandpaper, #600 fine-grit
Sponge brushes

INSTRUCTIONS

Prepare Surface:
1. Refer to Preparing Surfaces on page 14. Prepare clay pot.

2. Using sponge brush, base-coat pot with several coats Taffy, sanding between coats. Let dry.

3. Using a slip-slap motion, cover pot with Raw Sienna and Sunflower. Let dry.

Prepare & Adhere Prints:
1. Refer to Preparing Prints for Découpage on page 15. Cut out chicken motifs. Separate and discard inner layers.

2. Refer to Applying Prints on pages 16–17. Using sponge brush, adhere cutouts onto pot with découpage finish.
Let dry.

Finish:
1. Cover entire pot with two coats découpage finish.
Let dry.

Note: If using clay pots for plants, it is recommended to use a plastic liner between plant and inside of pot.

Chicken
Pot
Instructions begin
on page 117

Découpage designs can be used to create holiday accents, ornaments, and fabulous gift boxes that can be used year after year. The following pages show a variety of ideas and techniques.

Victorian Santa Ornaments

Pictured on page 120

Designed by
Chris Adams, SCD

GATHER THESE SUPPLIES

Surface:
Plastic foam balls, 3" dia. (2)

Prints:
Paper doilies, cream
Paper cutouts of Victorian
   Santas
Sheet music
Tissue papers:
   Green
   Red

Other Supplies:
Acrylic craft paints:
   Antique Gold
   Inca Gold
   Silver Sterling
   Solid Bronze
Acrylic sealer spray
Découpage finish
Embellishments:
   Artificial berries & fir
   Miniature pinecones
   Tiny gold jingle bells

Gold braid
Gold glitter
Hot-glue gun & glues sticks
Sea sponge
Sponge brushes

INSTRUCTIONS

Prepare Surface:
1. Refer to Preparing Surfaces on page 14. Prepare balls.

Prepare & Adhere Prints:
1. Refer to Preparing Prints for Découpage on page 15. Cut doilies and sheet music into pieces.

2. Refer to Applying Prints on pages 16–17. Using sponge brush, adhere red and green tissue papers onto balls with découpage finish. Use tissue scraps to cover any bald spots. Let dry.

3. Refer to Sponging Background on page 20. Using damp sponge, sponge balls with Antique Gold, Silver Sterling, and Solid Bronze. Let dry.

4. Using sponge brush, adhere pieces of doily, sheet music, and Santa cutouts onto balls with découpage finish. Let dry.

5. Using damp sponge, sponge Inca Gold over Santas for aged look.

6. Using sponge brush, cover balls with two coats découpage finish. On second coat, quickly drop glitter onto balls as you work. Let dry.

7. Cover balls with découpage finish to seal. Let dry.

Finish:
1. Spray balls with acrylic sealer.

2. Refer to Adding 3-D Accents on page 20. Using hot-glue gun, adhere gold braid around circumference of balls, joining ends at top and leaving one side longer to make loop for hanging ornament.

3. Arrange and adhere bells, berries, and pinecones onto top of ornaments.

Victorian Santa
Ornaments
Instructions begin
on page 119

Gift Boxes

Pictured on page 122

Designed by
Kathi Malarchuk Bailey

GATHER THESE SUPPLIES

Surface:
Papier-maché boxes,
  hexagonal, 3", 5", 7"

Prints:
Metallic tissue paper
Poinsettia print tissue paper

Other Supplies:
Cellulose sponge, 1" square
Découpage finish
Gold foil kit
Gold wire-edged ribbon
Sponge brush

INSTRUCTIONS

Prepare Surface:
1. Refer to Preparing Surfaces on page 14. Prepare boxes.

Prepare & Adhere Prints:
1. Cut paper pieces for boxes twice the required size for wrinkled look.

2. Refer to Applying Prints on pages 16–17. Using sponge brush, cover boxes with découpage finish, then press, push, and slide papers over surfaces. Let dry 30 minutes.

3. Tear and adhere scraps of paper over first coat of paper for dimensional look. Cut pieces to fit bottoms.

4. Cover boxes with découpage finish and press paper to surface. Let dry.

Apply Gold Foil:
1. Using sponge, apply foil kit adhesive to boxes. Let dry until clear.

2. Apply gold foil over adhesive, following manufacturer's instructions.

3. Using applicator tip, outline images on medium box.

Finish:
1. Using sponge brush, cover boxes and lids with two coats découpage finish to seal. Let dry.

2. Stack boxes and tie with gold ribbon.

Frosted Ornaments

Pictured on page 122

Designed by
Lauren Powell

GATHER THESE SUPPLIES

Surface:
Plastic foam balls, 3" dia.

Prints:
Holiday print paper napkins

Other Supplies:
Christmas picks
Clear crystal glitter
Clear plastic bag
Découpage finish
Gold cord
Hot-glue gun & glue sticks
Ribbon
Sponge brushes

INSTRUCTIONS

Prepare Surface:
1. Refer to Preparing Surfaces on page 14. Prepare balls.

Prepare & Adhere Prints:
1. Refer to Preparing Prints for Découpage on page 15. Cut out several holiday motifs. Tear several napkins into small pieces. Separate and discard inner layers.

2. Refer to Applying Prints on pages 16–17. Using sponge brush, adhere napkin pieces onto balls with découpage finish.

Finish:
1. Pour glitter in plastic bag. Cover ball with découpage finish until wet. Drop ball in bag to coat with glitter. Remove and let dry.

2. Repeat with remaining balls.

3. Refer to Adding 3-D Accents on page 20. Using hot-glue gun, adhere gold cord around circumference of balls, joining ends at top and leaving one side longer to make loop for hanging ornament.

Gift Boxes
Instructions begin
on page 121

Frosted
Ornaments
Instructions begin on page 121

Snowman Plate

Pictured on page 124

Designed by
Lauren Powell

GATHER THESE SUPPLIES

Surface:
Glass plate, 10" dia.

Print:
Snow family print

Other Supplies:
Acrylic craft paints:
   Blue Ink
   Red Light
   Wicker White
Brayer
Brushes:
   #6 Flat
   #10 Flat
   Liner
   Sponge(s)
Découpage finish
Paper towels
Rubbing alcohol
Small natural sponge

INSTRUCTIONS

Prepare Surface:
1. Refer to Preparing Surfaces on page 14. Prepare plate.

2. Using paper towels, clean plate with rubbing alcohol.

Prepare & Adhere Print:
1. Refer to Preparing Prints for Découpage on page 15. Cut out snow family motif.

2. Refer to Reverse Découpaging on page 19. Using sponge brush, adhere front of cutout onto plate back center with découpage finish. Using brayer, smooth cutout to remove air bubbles. Let dry.

3. Using sponge brush, cover plate back center with découpage finish. Let dry.

Paint:
1. Using sponge, lightly cover plate back center area with Wicker White. Let dry.

2. Using liner, paint stripe on plate back rim ⅜" from center area with Blue Ink.

3. Using #6 flat brush, paint stripe ⅜" from narrow stripe and center area with Blue Ink.

4. Using #10 flat brush, paint stripes on rim with Red Light.

5. Paint rim with Wicker White. Let dry.

Finish:
1. Using sponge brush, cover entire plate back with découpage finish. Let dry.

Snowman Ornaments

Pictured on page 124

Designed by
Marianne Ajamy

GATHER THESE SUPPLIES

Surface:
Plastic foam balls, 3" dia. (2)

Print:
Snowman print paper napkins

Other Supplies:
Acrylic craft paint:
   Pure Gold
Brushes:
   Liner
   Sponge
Découpage finish
Flocking adhesive
Floral wire, 5" (2)
Gold glitter
Hot-glue gun & glue sticks
Jingle bells
Ribbon
Thin metallic cord
White flocking

INSTRUCTIONS

Prepare Surface:
1. Refer to Preparing Surfaces on page 14. Prepare balls.

Prepare & Adhere Prints:
1. Refer to Preparing Prints for Découpage on page 15. Cut out snowman motifs. Separate and discard inner layers.

2. Push wire into balls to make hanger for ornaments and to use as handles while working.

3. Refer to Applying Prints on pages 16–17. Using sponge brush, cover balls with découpage finish. Press on cutouts. Let dry.

Finish:
1. Cover one ball around snowman with flocking adhesive. Pour on flocking fibers. Let dry.

2. Using liner, outline motifs with Pure Gold. Let dry.

3. Cover remaining ball around cutout with découpage finish. While wet, roll ball in glitter. Let dry.

4. Refer to Adding 3-D Accents on page 20. Using hot-glue gun, adhere cords, ribbons, and bells onto ornaments.

Snowman Plate
Instructions begin
on page 123

Snowman
Ornaments
Instructions begin
on page 123

Product Sources

FolkArt® Acrylic Colors:
High-quality brush-on acrylic paints. They are premixed colors available in 170 hues. Clean-up is easy with soap and water.

Autumn Leaves, #920
Baby Blue, #442
Basil Green, #645
Blue Ink, #642
Blue Ribbon, #719
Bluebell, #909
Bright Peach, #682
Coastal Blue, #713
Dark Brown, #416
Dove Gray, #708
Emerald Isle, #647
French Blue, #639
French Vanilla, #431
Fresh Foliage, #954
Leaf Green, #447
Lemon Custard, #735
Licorice, #938
Light Periwinkle, #640
Linen, #420
Lipstick Red, #437
Medium Gray, #425
Mushroom, #472
Old Ivy, #927
Olive Green, #449
Patina, #444
Periwinkle, #404
Purple, #411
Purple Passion, #638
Rose Chiffon, #753
Summer Sky, #906
Sunflower, #432
Taffy, #825
Tapioca, #903

Tartan Green, #725
Teal Green, #733
Teddy Bear Tan, #419
Wicker White, #901

FolkArt Artists' Pigments™:
Asphaltum, #476
Brilliant Ultramarine, #484
Burnt Sienna, #943
Burnt Umber, #462
Medium Yellow, #455
Pure Black, #479
Red Light, #629
Warm White, #649
Yellow Light, #918
Yellow Ochre, #917

FolkArt® Metallic Colors:
Antique Copper, #666
Antique Gold, #658
Copper, #664
Inca Gold, #676
Pure Gold, #660
Sahara Gold Metallic, #577
Silver Sterling, #662
Solid Bronze, #663

Apple Barrel® Craft Paints:
Aqua Marine, #20774
Green Clover, #20776
Neon Yellow, #20490

Royal Coat® Découpage Finish:
Glues and seals projects for a smooth, hard, satin finish. Available in 8-oz. (#1401), 16-oz. (#1402), and one gallon (#1404) sizes.

Royal Coat® Antique Découpage Finish: Creates a gentle, time-worn look. #1462

Mod Podge All-in-One Sealer, Glue, and Finish: Available in matte or gloss finishes, as well as, a variety of sizes, ranging from 4-oz. to one gallon.

Plaid® Picture This Photo Transfer Medium: Water-based and nontoxic photograph transfer medium compatible with color or black-and-white photographs. Available in opaque 4-oz. (#24901) and 8-oz. (#24902) sizes or clear 4-oz. (#24912) and 8-oz. (#24913) sizes.

Royal Coat® Treasure Gold: A metallic wax formula which adds gold accents quickly and easily. Classic Gold, #1459

Royal Coat™ Découpage Foil Kit: For dimensional gold accents with the look of gold leafing. #1422

FolkArt® Crackle Medium: Gives a weathered and time-worn finish to projects. Available in 2-oz. (#694), 4-oz. (#695), and 8-oz. (#696) sizes.

FolkArt® Glazing Medium:
Unique three-in-one product stains, antiques, and faux-finishes. Available in 2-oz. (#693) and 8-oz. (#991) sizes.

FolkArt® Pearlizing Medium:
Brush on projects to add beautiful, translucent highlights. Available in 2-oz. (#487) size.

FolkArt® Clearcote Glaze:
Gives projects a lacquer-like, high-gloss finish. Available in 6-oz. (#784) and 11-oz. (#785) sizes.

FolkArt® Clearcote Matte Acrylic Sealer:
Gives projects a soft, matte finish. Available in 6-oz. (#788) and 12-oz. (#789) sizes.

FolkArt® Antiquing Medium:
Down Home Brown, #811

Decorator Blocks®:
Ivy, #53202
Little Garden Flowers,
    #53219

Decorator Stamps:
Acanthus Leaf, #53609
Casablanca, #53601
Tasha (medallion design),
    #53603

Plaid's Simply® Stencils:
Fleur-de-Lis Collection,
    #28171
Pretty in Pictures, #28035
Primitive Icons, #28040
Skins, #28915

Stencil Décor® Stencils:
Grapes, #27711

Stencil Décor® Tools:
Stencil Brushes, ¼", ½"

Stencil Décor® Stencil Gels:
Deep Purple, #26114
Fern, #26123
Twig, #26128
Wild Ivy, #26126

Stencil Décor® Dry-Brush Stencil Paint:
Truffles Brown, #26206

Decorator Products Tools:
Chamois Tool, #30130
Spatter Tool, #30121
Sea Sponge

Metric Conversion Chart

MM-Millimetres   CM-Centimetres

INCHES TO MILLIMETRES AND CENTIMETRES

INCHES	MM	CM	INCHES	CM	INCHES	CM
⅛	3	0.3	9	22.9	30	76.2
¼	6	0.6	10	25.4	31	78.7
½	13	1.3	12	30.5	33	83.8
⅝	16	1.6	13	33.0	34	86.4
¾	19	1.9	14	35.6	35	88.9
⅞	22	2.2	15	38.1	36	91.4
1	25	2.5	16	40.6	37	94.0
1¼	32	3.2	17	43.2	38	96.5
1½	38	3.8	18	45.7	39	99.1
1¾	44	4.4	19	48.3	40	101.6
2	51	5.1	20	50.8	41	104.1
2½	64	6.4	21	53.3	42	106.7
3	76	7.6	22	55.9	43	109.2
3½	89	8.9	23	58.4	44	111.8
4	102	10.2	24	61.0	45	114.3
4½	114	11.4	25	63.5	46	116.8
5	127	12.7	26	66.0	47	119.4
6	152	15.2	27	68.6	48	121.9
7	178	17.8	28	71.1	49	124.5
8	203	20.3	29	73.7	50	127.0

YARDS TO METRES

YARDS	METRES	YARDS	METRES	YARDS	METRES	YARDS	METRES	YARDS	METRES
⅛	0.11	2⅛	1.94	4⅛	3.77	6⅛	5.60	8⅛	7.43
¼	0.23	2¼	2.06	4¼	3.89	6¼	5.72	8¼	7.54
⅜	0.34	2⅜	2.17	4⅜	4.00	6⅜	5.83	8⅜	7.66
½	0.46	2½	2.29	4½	4.11	6½	5.94	8½	7.77
⅝	0.57	2⅝	2.40	4⅝	4.23	6⅝	6.06	8⅝	7.89
¾	0.69	2¾	2.51	4¾	4.34	6¾	6.17	8¾	8.00
⅞	0.80	2⅞	2.63	4⅞	4.46	6⅞	6.29	8⅞	8.12
1	0.91	3	2.74	5	4.57	7	6.40	9	8.23
1⅛	1.03	3⅛	2.86	5⅛	4.69	7⅛	6.52	9⅛	8.34
1¼	1.14	3¼	2.97	5¼	4.80	7¼	6.63	9¼	8.46
1⅜	1.26	3⅜	3.09	5⅜	4.91	7⅜	6.74	9⅜	8.57
1½	1.37	3½	3.20	5½	5.03	7½	6.86	9½	8.69
1⅝	1.49	3⅝	3.31	5⅝	5.14	7⅝	6.97	9⅝	8.80
1¾	1.60	3¾	3.43	5¾	5.26	7¾	7.09	9¾	8.92
1⅞	1.71	3⅞	3.54	5⅞	5.37	7⅞	7.20	9⅞	9.03
2	1.83	4	3.66	6	5.49	8	7.32	10	9.14

Index